ACCLAIM FOR
PIGGY BANKS TO PAYCHECKS

"Whether you deal with numbers every day like I do or are afraid of math, if you have kids, you need this book. It will give you the tools and techniques you need to set them well on their way to a satisfying life of money well spent."

~ DAVID TRAHAIR, AUTHOR OF *GET OFF YOUR ASSETS: ERASE DEBT, SAVE CASH, RETIRE RICH*

"Education and learning can be two vastly different things. An education about money and finances can be imposed on you from all aspects of life, from formal classes at schools, to the ups and downs of the economic markets, to how you negotiate your first lunch trade at primary school...Learning these life skills is essential to the well being of any individual. Mohr offers a wonderful, easy-to-read book that provides a family-friendly approach to finances for both parents and teachers to help kids build a solid financial foundation. It promotes life long learning and a great guide to supporting financially literate children. I strongly recommend it."

~ DR. ALISON SAMMEL, SCHOOL OF EDUCATION AND PROFESSIONAL STUDIES, GRIFFITH UNIVERSITY, QUEENSLAND, AUSTRALIA

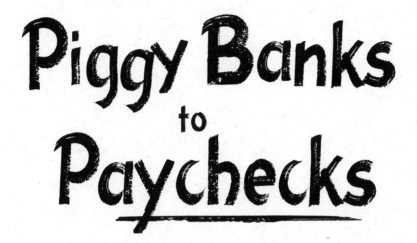

Piggy Banks
to
Paychecks

Helping kids understand
the value of a dollar

Piggy Banks to Paychecks

Helping kids understand the value of a dollar

ANGIE MOHR CA, CMA

Author of the *Numbers 101 for Small Business* series

Published in Canada by Fitzhenry & Whiteside,
195 Allstate Parkway, Markham, ON L3R 4T8

Published in the United States by Fitzhenry & Whiteside,
311 Washington Street, Brighton, Massachusetts 02135

Printed in Canada.
10 9 8 7 6 5 4 3 2 1
Fitzhenry & Whiteside acknowledges with thanks the Canada Council for the
Arts, and the Ontario Arts Council for their support of our publishing program.
We acknowledge the financial support of the Government of Canada through the
Canada Book Fund (CBF) for our publishing activities.

 Canada Council Conseil des Arts
for the Arts du Canada
 ONTARIO ARTS COUNCIL
CONSEIL DES ARTS DE L'ONTARIO

Library and Archives Canada Cataloguing in Publication
Mohr, Angie
Piggy banks to paychecks : helping kids understand
the value of a dollar / Angie Mohr.
Includes bibliographical references and index.
ISBN 978-1-55455-210-8
1. Children--Finance, Personal. I. Title.
HG179.M575 2011 332.0240083 C2011-907144-4
United States Library of Congress Cataloging-in-Publication Data
Mohr, Angie
Piggy banks to paychecks : helping kids understand
the value of a dollar / Angie Mohr.
[ ] p. : ill. ; cm.
Includes bibliographical references and index.
Summary: A practical approach for parents to help their children learn the critical
money skills, such as earning and saving money, budgeting, understanding
taxes, and running a business. Each chapter tackles a different skill; and includes
worksheets and checklists to help parents and children.
ISBN: 978-1-55455-210-8 (pbk.)
1. Children —Finance, Personal . I. Title.
332.0240083 dc23 PHG179.M647 2011

DEDICATION

This book is dedicated to all of the parents out there who stay up late at night worrying about their finances and about how their children will fare in the financial world of the future. There is a path forward, no matter what your current situation. Giving your children the gift of a financial education is important, if not always glamorous. You have the will and, now, the tools to ensure that they grow up money smart. My best to your family!

CONTENTS

NOTICE TO READERS

ACKNOWLEDGMENTS

There are so many people who recognize the importance of this topic and were ardent supporters of this book right from the beginning.

I would like to start by thanking my publisher, Fitzhenry & Whiteside, for performing the role of midwife to the book. Also, huge thanks to my agent, Hilary McMahon, of Westwood Creative Artists.

There are many people who work incredibly hard in the service of teaching financial literacy. So many parents, teachers, and other mentors take the time to share the financial basics with children, who will grow up to be money-wise adults. I am also grateful to others who work to officially change the way financial literacy is taught in schools and offered to adults. In particular, I would like to thank Donald Stewart and Evelyn Jacks of Canada's federal Task Force on Financial Literacy and Gail Vaz-Oxlade, Ellen Roseman, and David Trahair who continue to help consumers destroy debt, invest wisely, and lead fiscally calm and immensely satisfying lives.

I also have such deep gratitude to those from across North America who shared their personal family money stories with me and with all of the readers of this book. Their candid stories appear throughout the book.

Lastly, I want to thank my children, Alex and Erika, for being willing participants in our family's financial teaching travails. And, no, this doesn't mean your allowance is going up.

LYNN'S STORY

I think I have taught my children quite a bit of financial knowledge. They both know the importance of saving and budgeting. On my daughter's 18th birthday, we started an RRSP for her and plan to do the same for my son when he turns 18. I'm sure there will be things that come along in the future that I will wish I had told them, but, for now, I think they both have a very educated understanding of money.

My children never really had an allowance growing up. They knew that not every shopping trip was a trip for them to come home with something. Once in awhile they were treated if their behavior was acceptable. As they got a bit older, they were given money as needed-e.g., if their friends wanted to go to the movies or out for food, etc. Money was not thrown around frivolously by any means, but neither of my children wanted for much and, luckily, both have come to appreciate the freedoms they were allowed.

Each of my children had a savings account opened for them shortly after birth. Any money from birthdays, Christmas, and the Government went into these accounts. Once they were old enough to get a job, I asked them to put "some" of their paychecks into this account each payday. I told them it did not have to be a lot, but the more they put into the account, the more it would benefit them later on.

My daughter babysat from time to time, but both of my children got actual jobs at the age of 16. My daughter kept the same job until she went off to college. My son just turned 16 and has acquired his first part-time job this summer. So far, so good for him.

My husband and I differ in our opinions about whether our kids would be allowed to move back in with us when they get older. I love my children to death and always want them to be around. He believes that you should be out on your own at 18 or so. We do agree on the idea that if you have to move back in but are going to school, there will be no rent, but you will help around the house. If you have a job and need a place to stay while you save up for your own, then "some" rent will be put in place as well as still helping out around the house. My children have always been very good with their money. My daughter, being the thriftier one, would comparison shop, wait for sales, or hope Mom would buy it out of niceness. Her spending would be on smaller items such as clothing and aesthetics. My son always has his eye on the BIG things and would/will save his money until he has enough for that one special purchase.

~ LYNN G., INNISFIL, ONTARIO

CHAPTER ONE

Raising Money Smart Kids

✓ WHY I WROTE THIS BOOK

I have to start out by admitting that both my children find it absolutely hysterical that I am writing a book on teaching kids about money. It's certainly not that I don't have the professional background to do it. I am a Chartered Accountant and Certified Management Accountant and have worked with more than a thousand clients on tax, accounting, and personal finance issues. I have had many columns and articles featured in high-profile magazines and newspapers and I write regularly for finance Web sites, such as Motley Fool, Investopedia, Forbes, the Globe and Mail, and MSNBC Money. I've even had the pleasure of working with some famous clients, from celebrity chefs to rock bands.

Why, then, do my kids giggle when I tell them I'm working on this book? The truth is, teaching kids how to view, handle, and accumulate money is one of the hardest jobs out there. Every family is different and has differing views on what money lessons need to be passed on. It's not something that happens overnight. And it's never a smooth process.

In our family, we have gone through many iterations of this process. We have tried the flat rate allowance, the tough-love "save it all" version, and have finally settled into more natural, daily experiences with money that allow the kids to test out their fiscal wings in a somewhat sheltered atmosphere. I'm proud of how much my children know about earning, spending, saving, budgeting, and other financial subjects. Like everyone else, they are still bound to make money mistakes in their lifetime, but they will have the tools at their disposal to get themselves back on course.

"Money is like a sixth sense-and you can't make use of the other five without it"
~William Somerset Maugham

The main reason I wrote this book, however, was for all of the parents out there who know in their hearts that they need to put their kids on the right financial path but are afraid. You may fear that you have made too many money mistakes yourself to be able to share anything useful with your kids. You may fear that you'll teach them bad habits or fail to teach them critical money lessons. You may want to leave the lessons up to teachers and bankers and other "professionals."

The truth is that you have to be the one to guide your children. It's both your responsibility and your privilege. Although it is encouraging that there is a growing movement in schools to include some financial literacy curriculum, it is ultimately up to you to give your kids the tools to handle money that will benefit them their whole lives. What about the fear that you don't know enough of the important stuff to share? First, there are many resources out there to help you find your way. This book is meant to be one of them. Second, children learn as much from their parents' mistakes as from their successes. Don't be afraid to show your kids where you have strayed from the path. Let them know that it's okay to not do everything perfectly. There's always a road back to financial stability and wealth. Everyone's road looks a little different and that may be the most important financial lesson you ever teach your kids.

It doesn't matter how old your children are or how difficult your financial situation is at the moment. It doesn't matter which money lessons you start with. It doesn't matter what kind of allowance system you choose to set up with your kids. It only matters that you get started right now, with the tools you have to work with and the knowledge you already have. If you're unsure as to how much you do know, there is a quiz at the end of Chapter Two to help you focus on your weak areas.

Giving your kids a financial education will be one of the most important things you do as a parent. Jump in. Your kids will thank you for it.

How to Read This Book

Every family will have different prior experiences with financial knowledge. Your kids may already know all about saving or budgeting, for example. Feel free to jump around in the book and read the pieces that are most important to your family. Eventually, however, everyone will benefit from a review of the basics. You may get a new perspective on certain money management issues. Or you may surprise yourself by how much you already know. I hope that you use this book as a resource that you can come back to time and again to brush up on your skills and find new ways to help your children get money savvy.

If there are terms in this book with which you are not familiar, there is a glossary, called "Money Words," at the end of the book with definitions of many of the financial terms in this book along with other common terms you will come across while teaching your kids money skills.

For more information on helping kids understand money concepts, join me over at *www. piggybanks2paychecks.com* for downloadable worksheets, more money games, and even financial lesson plans. Use the "Contact Angie" button to send me your money stories and share your experiences.

When I was growing up, my parents never talked about money in front of us kids. I didn't know until after my father passed away that it was because we didn't have any money. I think my parents thought that they could hide that from us—and they did a very good job of it. I never felt like I was deprived of anything, although I never got as much at Christmas as most of my friends. I sort of felt like maybe Santa didn't like me as much as them. But we got by and had lots of family time together. My mom and dad scraped together the house mortgage payment every month and kept the lights on, so we didn't know any differently. I wish they had taught us those money skills, though, so that my siblings and I didn't have to learn them the hard way through experience.

~ HAROLD D., VANCOUVER, BRITISH COLUMBIA

The Language of Piggy Banks to Paychecks

As you might imagine, it's quite a chore to produce a financial book that is relevant to both Canadians and Americans. There are differences in the banking and tax systems and the way the economy works. I have included both throughout and it is my hope that you find reading about the differences enlightening.

I did, however, have to choose a "language" for the book. There are spelling differences between the two countries. The first you will notice is in the title itself. "Paycheck" is the American version of the Canadian "Paycheque." Ultimately, I chose to use American spelling throughout, mainly because most of the financial literature Canadians are exposed to use American spelling, including most Canadian newspapers.

> "If you want to feel rich, just count the things you have that money can't buy"
> ~ Proverb

✓ A WORD ABOUT MONEY PHILOSOPHY

How you treat money and how you handle it are dependent on many factors, some of them non-financial. Everyone has a different philosophy of the role money and wealth play in their lives. You may have learned your philosophy about money from your parents or grandparents or simply developed your financial attitudes as you became more experienced in your lifetime. Some people would never consider borrowing a single dollar from anyone else. Some believe that having lots of debt will ultimately make them the most income. Some forego spending money on vacations and entertainment today in order to have more when they retire. And some decided long ago to live in the moment and worry about their financial futures later.

While there are some definite incorrect ways to handle your finances, there is no right or wrong philosophy. You will teach your children money skills based on your own beliefs. When they are older and living on their own, they will have to decide for themselves how much of your philosophy to adopt. All you can do is teach your children to the best of your ability and let them find their own path in life—and that is applicable to more than just money skills. Be prepared that your children may grow up, leave the house, and handle their money very differently than you do. As long as they have the basic tools at their disposal to guide them, they will be fine. And so will you.

✓ WHY KIDS NEED TO LEARN MONEY SKILLS

Think back to your school days. What subjects did you learn in the classroom? Reading, writing, and math for sure. History, geography, and science as you progressed through the grades. Perhaps even art and music. All of these subjects are important and certainly useful to you at some point in your life (even though you probably swore up and down when you were eleven that you would never have any practical use for algebra!).

> "Whoever said money can't buy happiness simply didn't know where to go shopping."
> ~ Bo Derek

The one subject that is usually not taught in the school system is the one that will have a huge impact on your life each and every day: money. How to earn it, spend it, invest it, and pass it on to the next generation.

There are many colloquial sayings about money:

"Money is the root of all evil"

"Money can't buy happiness"

"Money talks"

None of these phrases paints money in a favorable light. It is true that the pursuit of money has caused famine, war, and even death. However, the inability to manage money:

- Is the number one cause of divorce in North America.
- Is responsible for the astronomical jump in personal bankruptcies in the past decade.
- Perpetuates generational poverty.
- Leads to stress, poor health, and poor self-image.

As you can see, the subject of money is far-reaching and controversial. It can impact our lives in many different ways. Our understanding of money can be the difference between having financial abundance in our lives and simply scraping by.

If money is so important, why isn't it being taught in our school systems? There are probably as many answers to that question as there are educators, but one of the major reasons is that money is seen as a commercial rather than an academic subject.

Whatever the reasons, the fact that the subject of money is not taught in schools simply means that it must be taught at home. In many families, however, there are reasons why financial savvy is not being passed from generation to generation:

- Parents feel like they have never learned the skills to manage money themselves, much less be able to teach their children.

- They feel that talking about money with their children is crass. "Good" families don't discuss income or wealth or unpaid bills.
- They are afraid that discussing money will scare the children and make them fearful that they are "poor."
- They are embarrassed about the family's financial situation and are afraid that their children will see what terrible money managers they have been.

All of these reasons are rooted in the traditions that parents have been raised in. If these fears are not overcome, the end result is that their children in elementary school learn about money the same way they do about sex and drugs: from friends, television, and what they perceive their parents are doing.

For example, I never knew how much my family members were earning at their jobs or making in their businesses. We were raised not to discuss such matters. Money was a very private subject, second only to sex in the "don't ask, don't tell" category. Consequently, growing up, I had no idea how much groceries cost or what it took to operate a car. I didn't know that you had to save money to be able to pay for university or to get by when you retire.

When children have to learn about finances from what they perceive that their parents are doing, they will likely end up forming some inaccurate pictures of their parents' money management. They may also be picking up their parents' bad money habits, which, eventually, they will pass on to their own children.

✓ THE SIX BAD MONEY HABITS KIDS LEARN FROM THEIR PARENTS

① I'm too young (too busy, too old, too whatever) to create a Lifetime Financial Plan.

Thinking about retirement may make you think about being "old"—something that many people don't want to contemplate. Retirement—one of the final stages of the Lifetime Financial Plan—may also seem unfathomably far away ("I've got lots of time to plan for that") or painfully close at hand ("It's too late for me to do anything about it now"). Financial planning for your retirement, though, is really only one segment of your Lifetime Financial Plan. Everyone should have a Lifetime Financial Plan, whether it's a carefully constructed set of computer spreadsheets or simply some figures jotted down on a scrap piece of paper. Your plan is your road map. It's how to get from HERE to THERE, or, more accurately, how to get from NOW to THEN. The plan addresses much more than retirement. It is a step-by-step guide to any financial goal. It answers the questions "How will we send the kids to university?" and "How can we buy that boat we've been looking at?" Teaching your kids to set up their own financial plans can help them cut their teeth on smaller goals, such as, "How long will it take me to save for that bicycle?" and "How many hours do I have to work at my summer job to earn $X?" Financial planning should be a regular and ongoing part of your life and the lives of your children.

② Let's buy it now and pay later.

We've all seen the ads on TV, the radio, and in newspapers and magazines:

"No money down and no payments until 2012!"

"Put it on your store credit card and make no payments for 12 months."

"No money? No problem! Instant credit approval."

Fifty years ago, most people had different views on purchasing than people do today. They were a generation of savers. If you wanted to buy something, you had to wait and put money away for it. They knew that something worth having was worth waiting for. Houses were purchased for cash or with large down payments. One rode a bicycle until he or she could save up enough to buy a car. Consumer debt loads were a fraction of what they are today. Personal bankruptcy was almost unheard of.

Now the power of mass media has taken root in society. Consumer products manufacturers understand the power of advertising to drive product demand and desire. Every university student in the country is inundated with offers for credit cards, new cars, and electronic equipment. It has become far too easy and socially acceptable to rack up backbreaking quantities of debt before a student is out of her twenties. When this new relaxed attitude toward debt is coupled with disappearing job stability, it spells disaster. In Canada alone, over 85,000 people declare personal bankruptcy every year, and between 1990 and 2010, consumer bankruptcies increased by over 116%. In the United States, the picture is even grimmer: 1.5 million people filed for personal bankruptcy in 2010, a 9% increase from the prior year.

Our children need to be able to sift through the mountains of advertising hype they are bombarded with on a daily basis and make informed, calculated consumer decisions.

There will always be more money where that came from.

Once upon a time, all you had to do to be financially set for life was to get a job with the right company. Your employment would be secure and your salary would steadily increase until your retirement at age 65, at which point, you would walk out the door with a gold watch and a significant pension that would more than fund your twilight years.

Those days are long gone. Job stability and the concept of "lifetime employment" have declined steadily with the globalization of trade and emerging technologies. What it once took an entire city block of keypunch operators to accomplish in a day can now be handled by a desktop computer in a nanosecond. Companies are downsizing their workforce to stay competitive not only with companies in their town but also with competition on the other side of the world. Employees have become like nomads, staying in one position only until the spring runs dry. This has an impact on workers' earnings as well as their pensions. Employment income can no longer be viewed as a never-ending river of dollars, but as a precious resource that needs to be preserved.

④ *I don't have enough money to bother investing.*

This is perhaps one of the weakest arguments for bad financial stewardship. It is a circular argument. The reason there isn't enough money is that it hasn't been invested, not the other way around. It is always better to save a little than to save nothing. Investment plans can be set up with as little as $10 a month. Every little bit helps. Remember that oceans are made up of tiny drops of water collected together.

"Formal education
will make you a living;
self-education will make
you a fortune."
~ Jim Rohn

⑤ *Only poor people have to prepare and stick to a budget.*

In the ground-breaking book, *The Millionaire Next Door: The Surprising Secrets of America's Wealthy* (1996, Simon & Schuster Inc., New York) written by Thomas Stanley and William Danko, the authors set out to survey the habits and lifestyles of a representative segment of America's 3.5 million millionaire households. Among many other intriguing traits, they found that the majority of those millionaires adhere to a strict budget. They plan where every penny is going and they track their spending. Budgeting is what helps them become millionaires. You can't save what you don't track.

⑥ *I just don't have a head for numbers.*

If you've never had experience in taking control of your finances, it can seem overwhelming and perhaps beyond your skill level. That perception makes it easy to say, "I just can't do it" or "I was never very good at math." In truth, however, managing your financial situation takes only common sense and some easily learned tools (like those found in this book). It's not necessary to have a degree in accounting or finance to be able to plan your financial life.

According to the annual *Forbes Magazine* listing, as of March 2011, there are 1,210 billionaires in the world. The number of millionaires is approaching 10 million.

✓ WHY RICH KIDS NEED MONEY SKILLS EVERY BIT AS MUCH AS POOR KIDS

In the "Six Bad Money Habits" section above, we talked about the fact that millionaires engage in budgeting and financial planning activities as much or more so than less affluent people. Being able to retain wealth is as important as being able to accumulate it in the first place. We've all read newspaper stories about lottery winners who become instant millionaires overnight and end up broke and on welfare within a year because they were never taught how to care for and manage wealth.

More frequent but less reported stories abound on the flip side of the coin, where people who started with nothing, slowly and carefully amassed a great deal of wealth for themselves and future generations.

Affluent parents in particular need to teach their children how to retain wealth or else they risk their children viewing money as something to be taken for granted, something that will always be around. It's easier to place a high value on a scarce commodity rather than one that's lying around in abundance.

✓ MONEY LESSONS TRANSLATE INTO WIDER VALUE JUDGMENTS

One of the most important reasons to teach our children the value of money is to help them learn to hone their value assessments. When we make comparative judgments about something's monetary worth, we can use that same skill to judge non-monetary worth.

For example, the same skills are necessary to assess the following dilemmas:

① Jonathan is 15 years old. He has held an after-school job delivering newspapers for almost a year. Jonathan opened a bank account when he started his job and has managed to save almost $600. There are two things that Jonathan really wants to buy with his savings, but he can only buy one of them with his current bank balance. The first is a new Fender Stratocaster guitar, not the run-of-the-mill entry model, but the Eric Clapton Signature Strat. Jonathan has played in a band on weekends with a few of his school friends for two months now and he really wants to get a "proper" guitar. Cost: $575.

The second item that Jonathan has his eye on is a mountain bike. He's been doing research on the Internet and has found his perfect bike. It can be built and shipped to him for $395.

Jonathan will have to make a decision whether to just buy one item now, buy one now and continue to save up for the other one, or delay purchasing either item until he has enough for both (or until one goes on sale). The process he will use to determine the best solution for him will involve weighing the value of each item to him. Will he get more enjoyment out of the guitar or the bike? Will waiting on both garner him a more favorable price on the items? How sure is he that he won't find something he wants more in a few months and regret his purchase?

These assessments of the monetary value of these items will result in Jonathan's choosing how to spend his earned income in a way that is comfortable for him.

Jonathan also has a time dilemma. His math teacher has offered to spend an hour every Saturday afternoon with him for the rest of the school year to help him boost his math grades, which have consistently been in the lower half of the class all year. Jonathan knows that there are many benefits to higher math grades, including a better chance of eventually getting into the university he wants to attend. A better understanding and aptitude in math would also give him more immediate pleasure in not feeling so uncomfortable in his math class.

The problem is that this tutoring occurs at the same time as band practice. Neither can be easily moved. Jonathan has to decide which option holds more value for him. He will use the same value assessment tools as he used in the monetary spending decision he made with the guitar and the bike.

✓ TEACHING A CHILD TO FISH

As parents, we always want to make decisions for our children that will keep them safe and will protect them. In fact, that is our job: keeping them safe from harm and ensuring that they don't do anything in the short term that will harm them later in life.

We know from prior experience, for example, that if our child was to take his $20 birthday money from Grandma and spend it all on Pokemon trading cards, he will get enjoyment out of the purchase for about two days. Then, he will lose interest in the cards and they will eventually end up under his bed. That makes it easy for us to say "no" when asked. However, in the long run, it's more important to help our children come to that value judgment on their own. It may mean that they make some purchases that we wouldn't have chosen for them. It takes longer and requires more of us as parents, but we will be teaching our kids lifelong lessons about value that they will apply to various situations even after they have grown up and flown the coop. We will talk more about teaching children about spending in Chapter Six: "Paying the Piper."

The value of a solid financial education to our children is incalculably great. It not only gives them the tools they need to become financially grounded but also lets them pass our lessons along to their own children. Our next stop on this journey is to take a look at our own financial habits.

✓ BE A MONEY MENTOR TO YOUR KIDS' FRIENDS

When I was growing up, I spent most summers at my grandparents' house. My best friend lived across the road and we spent almost every waking minute together. My grandmother wasn't excited about loud, messy kids so we spent most of our time outside or at my friend's house. Sometimes, we would take off to the park or the woods on our bikes but, often, we would hang out at her house. Her father was an economics professor and her mother was an artist. It was a completely different world than the one I lived in and I learned so much from my friend's parents—lessons that have stayed with me until this day. They helped shape how I felt about education and following one's own path. I don't think they ever knew how deeply their presence affected me.

> I know I really should teach my daughter more about finances, but I guess I'm rather scared that she'll find out just how bad ours are. I don't want to scare her or have her worry that we won't be able to pay the rent. I think that's a burden a parent has to keep to oneself. On the other hand, I want to make sure that she gets off on the right foot and spends and saves her money wisely. I'm just not sure if I'm the right person to try to help her.
>
> ~ BETTY Y., BATON ROUGE, LOUISIANA

As adults, we affect not only our own children but also our children's friends. Just by being who you are and allowing your kids' friends to be around you, you provide them with new experiences and potentially with different ways of seeing the world.

With that in mind, what better gift can you give their friends than financial education? Most families do not discuss money at home, much less teach their children how to handle it. If you are already teaching your own children how to handle money, doing it in front of their friends can help them as well. It doesn't have to be any kind of formal training, but talking about your kids' savings plans, the household rules about earning money for allowance and saving it, and rules about spending, help other kids handle their own money better.

Most importantly, be there for your kids' friends if they have questions about money. They may have little concept of how finances work or they may even have a warped and dysfunctional view of how it works by observing what goes on in their own home. Take the time to answer their questions but don't lecture them. You're there as a resource, not an instructor.

> "What we really want to do is what we are really meant to do. When we do what we are meant to do, money comes to us, doors open for us, we feel useful, and the work we do feels like play to us."
> ~Julia Cameron

Whether you're conscious of it or not, you are a mentor to and an influence on not only your own kids but their friends, too. Give them a solid foundation in money management and they'll have those skills for a lifetime.

✓ SUMMARY

- Every family has its own money philosophy that works for it. Teach kids your way and let them decide as adults how much of your philosophy they want to carry into their own financial lives.

- The most important reason that kids need to learn money skills from you is that, if they have to figure it out on their own, they'll learn bits and pieces from television, movies, school friends, and from their own observations of your money habits. Early financial education helps to avoid misconceptions and mistakes down the road.

- Kids need financial literacy regardless of their family's wealth or lack thereof. They will learn from your wisdom, and also from your mistakes. Sharing your family's finances with your kids helps them learn about the good, the bad, and the ugly of your financial management.

- Solid money skills help kids with their comparative valuation skills, even in non-financial decisions. Teaching children how to assess two or more options and choose the one with the most benefits for the least risk will benefit them for the rest of their lives.

- You can be a positive financial influence on your child's friends also. Some families still do not talk about money at home. Let your house be a safe haven for kids to ask questions and learn.

KAY'S STORY

My daughter was given a weekly allowance. She was also expected to do chores as part of being a member of the family. The two were not related. She also had the option of earning money by doing special projects around the house. She started "working" in the family business when she was about three years old, going through moldy strawberries, and other fruit and picking out the bad stuff. I always included her in my work so she would understand about money and what it could and could not accomplish.

I set up a bank account for her before her 1st birthday. Money that she got for her birthday, etc., went in there. She learned to plan her purchases by saving her money and she was instructed to always pay herself first by putting 1/2 away of whatever she earned for the "future."

When she was really young and she wanted to buy something, I would go through the conversation, "Do you want it or need it." I asked questions to help her walk through her thoughts logically, saying, "Ok, if you buy that, and something else comes up, will you be in a position to buy the other thing?" I let her make choices, mistakes, and pay the consequences of her actions when she was 8 or 9. By the time she was 16, she already had a very good head on her shoulders about money. I thought she would ask for my help when she went to go buy a car at age 18, but she did it all on her own. She negotiated a great buy price on the car, great insurance, had established good credit, and was prepared with her big down payment. She had driven a clunker for two years to save up. I was very impressed with her ability to make good decisions and I'm glad I did it the way I did, involving her early and often. I've watched my friends spend a lot of wasted money on their kids, and still the kids ask for more and more. Not in my house. We live well, we have what we need, and we each work hard if we want something more. I think being open and honest with kids is the best way. People don't get to be millionaires by spending their money; they get it by saving their money. It is so simple and yet most cannot fathom it. I wanted to be a millionaire by the time I was 45, and I did it. There is no reason she cannot do the same thing. It's all about making good choices. Money doesn't make you happy, but it sure brings misery when there isn't enough to cover the basics. Living within your means isn't that difficult to do once you decide to live that way.

I shared everything about the family's financial situation with my daughter from an early age. She knows we have CDs, stock, 401(k), IRA, and an annuity. She also knows we have a year's worth of cash in the safe deposit box if we should need it. As a family, we made the decision to become debt-free after 9/11. She also knows I looked for an employer that would pay for my college and did 10 years there so that I could have a "free" MBA with no school loans. She has never asked me for money for luxury items. Since she was really little, I covered the necessities, and if she wanted anything extra, she was responsible for saving her money and buying it when she could afford it.

My daughter started working for extra money from me before she was five. She was probably about 10 when she started working for other family members and

12 when she started babysitting and doing filing/typing activities for friends and neighbors. She elected not to go to college, but I did pay for her trade school education. She wants to open her own business at age 24.

My daughter tried to live on her own when she was 22 but she wasn't making enough money. I was glad to have her back. She pays $300 a month rent plus she takes care of the laundry for the house and does her own dishes, cooks once in a while, and participates in household projects. I remember that at age 15, I was on my own. My mother started charging me $50/week rent when I was 12 (because she wanted me to watch my brother and sister but I didn't want to do it). As a result, I moved out at 15 when I could afford to live on my own. However, I had no social life. I worked 40 hours a week on top of going to school while my friends were out having fun. I am grateful she is smarter than I was, and has chosen to live off the "rents" for a little longer.

My daughter graduated high school early and I was prepared to help her by picking up her college tuition costs, but then she chose not to go. Since then, I have gotten laid off myself so I went from making 100K to about 24K a year. If she chooses to go back now, I would help her, but I would force her to kick in as well. Many people who are graduating college cannot find work. In all actuality, I would strongly encourage her to find an employer who will pay for the education, just as I did.

My daughter is now almost 24. She manages her own money, got herself a loan for her car, and she pays off her bills on time. I have instructed her to build up her credit by using her credit card and then paying off the balance right away to reduce or eliminate interest fees.

~ KAY B., HARTFORD, CONNECTICUT

CHAPTER TWO

The Pot & the Kettle: A Look at Our Own Financial Habits

✓ INTRODUCTION

Teaching kids how to be fiscally responsible is like teaching them how to knit or to build a birdhouse. It's one part instruction and four parts imitation. Kids learn most of their lessons about money from watching what others appear to be doing. One of the greatest influences is you as a parent. Kids pick up on your attitudes about money. Do you spend ten dollars a day on lattes and lottery tickets? Your kids watch you do it. Do you spend time in the grocery store, calculating which size of cereal is the better value? Kids watch you do that, too.

A common reason why many parents shy away from helping their kids learn about money is that they don't know how to handle it themselves. The first step in our kids' financial education is to take an honest look at our own money habits. Often, that look may be uncomfortable. For example, you may know that you don't have a set spending budget and that you should, but it may be easier for you to ignore it and splurge when you want to.

But you can't help kids grow their financial knowledge without having some yourself. It doesn't mean that you have to go and take a course (although, there are some great ones out there). Learning better financial habits can be as simple as reading a book (like this one). You don't have to instantly transform yourself into a personal finance expert, but getting your own finances on track helps both you and your kids. If they are going to emulate you, make sure you give them something worth emulating!

✓ WHAT MONEY MYTHS ARE YOU STILL CARRYING AROUND?

In the same way that our kids learn money habits by what they see us doing, we likely learned them the same way—from watching our parents. It's time to examine what we think we know about money and put our financial beliefs to the test. Do we really know as much as we think we do? How many of these common money myths are you still carrying around?

① *My banker knows best how to invest my money.*

> While it is fine to take some direction from your investment advisor or bank, only you know what's best for your situation. Keep in mind that many investment advisors work on commission, so you may find that you're invested in funds that gave them the best return, not you. Work with an independent advisor;

whether that is an experienced accountant or a financial consultant who doesn't work on commission, be active in your own money management.

② *If I spend less than I make, I don't need a budget.*

It's not enough to simply have fewer dollars going out of your wallet than coming in every month. You need to know where those dollars are going. Some of them should be earmarked for debt repayment, some for saving, and some for current spending. Budgeting ensures that you take care of all of the important financial decisions first.

③ *It's too late to start saving for my kids' college or university tuition now.*

Saving something is always better than saving nothing— always! You can't do anything about your past money habits but you can start better ones today. Even if you will only be able to save a portion of the total cost of college, it's better than having to find all the money when the tuition bill comes in.

④ *My house is my best investment.*

This is probably one of the oldest and most tenacious money myths in existence. For a good portion of the last century, it was true. As house prices rose, people began relying on capital gains in their house to support them in retirement. But, as we've all seen in the past few years, especially in the United States, houses don't always go up in value. The bubble has burst and the market has to find a new normal. The bottom line is this: Don't tie all of your money up in your house! Diversify your investments.

> "Money, if it does not bring you happiness, will at least help you be miserable in comfort."
> ~ Helen Gurley Brown

⑤ *I don't need an emergency fund as long as I have room on my credit card.*

Despite what some late night, high-leverage investment "gurus" try to tell you, having access to credit is not the same thing as having money tucked safely in the bank. Credit card limits can be cut at any time, leaving you scrambling if you have an emergency. An emergency fund gives you guaranteed access to funds should you need them.

⑥ *I don't claim some deductions on my taxes because I don't want to get audited.*

I've had several new tax clients tell me this over the years. Some accountants even tell their clients that. The fact is that you should claim every single deduction and credit you are eligible for. Never fear an audit. If you have the appropriate back-up paperwork, an audit is a breeze. The only people who should fear an audit are those with dark tax secrets to hide. And that's not you, right?

⊚ *My job is solid. I get a raise every year.*

Most people think their job is a sure thing, right up to the minute that they get a pink slip. While you may not be able to prevent a job loss, you can ensure that you have a softer landing. Make sure your skills are up-to-date; keep your finger on the pulse of your industry, for example: know who is getting hired, what new technologies are changing the industry, and what you will need to learn to move up the ladder. Then, even if you are let go, you have skills to be able to secure a new job more quickly. Treat your job as an investment that you have to protect.

I never really thought about having to talk to my kids about money. They get a fixed allowance every week and that's their spending money. I figured that they would learn all about budgeting and things like that in school. I finally sat down with the state's curriculum last month and realized that there is nothing in there about handling money. I don't understand why the schools wouldn't be teaching something as important as this.

~ KATIE R., LUSK, WYOMING

✓ ARE YOU HANDLING MONEY LIKE ROSEANNE?

In the ABC comedy, *Roseanne*, that ran from 1988 to 1997 (and is in perpetual re-runs), the title character was the matron of a blue-collar family just trying to get by. They lived paycheck to paycheck and made just enough to pay their bills. Every now and then, they would stumble on to some extra money, through a job bonus or gift from a relative. They always celebrated their windfall by spending it. Then, the next week, it was back to scraping by.

Although *Roseanne* was a fictional show, it illustrates how many people handle their money: tightening their belts in the lean times and spending more liberally in the good times. It is one of the main causes of paycheck-to-paycheck living. Cash windfalls should be carefully managed just like any other kind of income. Top up the emergency fund or pay down some debt. Invest in a few upgrades to your home that will pay you back almost right away in energy savings. But don't spend it all on "fun" things.

That doesn't mean that saving money is all about abstaining from life. Part of your budget should be for entertainment and fun pursuits. But spend judiciously in both good times and bad.

✓ A NAME FOR EVERY DOLLAR

A frequent complaint I've heard from clients is that they simply don't know where their money goes. They may start off the week with two twenty-dollar bills in their wallet and, by the end of the week, it has transformed into two quarters, a few nickels, and a rumpled dollar bill. When you don't have a plan for your cash, it has a habit of draining away without your being fully aware of it.

One of the most basic money traits your children will see is how you treat cash. If your child wants a treat in the store, do you rummage around in your purse to see if you have enough spare change? Is how much money you have on hand the deciding factor for you as to whether you will make a purchase or not? If the answer is yes, it means that you don't name each dollar, i.e., you don't have a specific purpose for all of your income.

The most important financial skill your child will learn from you is planning. Before money comes in the house, you should already know where it's going, either to budgeted spending, savings, or debt repayment. That doesn't mean that you can't buy treats for the kids in the grocery store. It just means that those treats should already be part of the budget.

Your children watch you more frequently than you are aware. Regardless of what you tell them about money, they will put more stock into how they see you handle it in real life. Make sure you're not giving them the message, "Do as I say, not as I do." If you want them to be financially responsible, you must be their main role model.

"The art is not in making money, but in keeping it"
~ Proverb

✓ THE LANGUAGE OF MONEY

How we talk about money—the words, the phrases, the attitudes—is just as important as what we say about money. It's the same with food. If you talk about food like it's a reward for good behavior or a comfort for a stressful day, those attitudes will color what you do with food and how much you eat. The words you use about food, such as "You deserve a big bowl of ice cream," will shape how your children view and talk about food. Just as bad food habits can be carried over from generation to generation, so can bad money habits.

Money is nothing but a facilitator of commerce. It does not have any magical properties that will make people happier, more positive, healthier, or wiser. While having enough wealth to live a fulfilling and satisfying life is a fantastic goal, it's not the money itself that gets us there. It's what we do with our money and how we handle it.

For the next week, listen consciously to the words you use when you talk about money every day. Do you talk about it as if it's something that just appears and disappears outside of your control? Do you discuss how you will reward yourself with a shopping trip after a hard work week or "splurge" on an expensive dinner out? Do you talk about your retirement account with comments like, "I'm not even going to look at it—the markets are so bad right now"? The words we use define how in control we feel about money.

> "Money is only a tool. It will take you wherever you wish, but it will not replace you as the driver."
> ~ Ayn Rand

Remember that children are sponges. They listen to us when we think they're doing other things. They absorb our attitudes about wealth, budgeting, and financial security. Controlling the way you talk about money is the first step in teaching your children positive financial lessons. Money is not the end goal and it is something that we can harness and control. We are not helpless in our financial journey. Everyone has the ability to take the reins and direct their financial situation in the right direction.

Here are some money phrases that are a great start to talking about money more positively:

- "Our budget gives us $100 this month to plan our entertainment."

- "Because we saved $50 on our groceries this month, we can take $25 of it and go to the amusement park."

- "The housing market is significantly down right now, but we're not buying or selling and can ride it out just fine."

- "Let's go through next year's budget again and see if we can find some savings so that we can go to Mexico in the winter."

- "Mary, you did a great job managing the bake sale and it showed in the amount of money you made."

- "The car is still in good running order, so we'll keep it for at least another year."

- "We received more back on our income tax returns than we expected. Let's work the extra into the budget."

- "You saved up for that iPod all on your own and then researched and found a better price than n you were expecting. Great job saving money!"

My school-age kids don't know much about our finances. They seem to think money grows on trees! I don't feel the need to share our mortgage and credit info with them at this time. Maybe when they are older.

~ VICKI H., PHILADELPHIA, PENNSYLVANIA

Note that all of these phrases denote that you are in control of your money. You know where it came from and where it's going. You have your money on a leash, not the other way around.

Watch your thoughts for they become words.
Watch your words for they become actions.
Watch your actions for they become habits.
Watch your habits for they become your character.
Watch your character for it becomes your destiny.

~ Ralph Waldo Emerson

✓ IT'S OKAY NOT TO BE PERFECT

Every person handles money differently. Some people can handle more risk than others and everyone's goals are different. And everyone makes mistakes. Everyone. One fear that I have heard from hundreds of clients over the years is that they are afraid they'll mess up their financial position worse than it already is if they make changes. It's a fear that can be debilitating and causes many people to pull their hat down over their eyes and not look at their financial situation at all.

The good news is that almost all financial moves, decisions, and choices are correctible if they turn out to be the wrong ones. You will likely make missteps on your journey to strengthen your own financial knowledge and teach your children how to be fiscally responsible. And that's okay. As long as you are heading in the right direction overall, it is normal to make course corrections along the way. Your kids will learn just as much from your financial mistakes as they will from your successes. It's okay not to be perfect.

✓ TEST YOUR MONEY-HANDLING KNOWLEDGE

Take this short quiz to see how money-wise you are. Knowing which areas you have weaknesses in will help you to focus in on specific areas of this book so that you can beef up your own financial knowledge and pass it on to your kids.

Economics

1. If you buy a set of sheets from a foreign online company and pay in the foreign currency, you will pay more when:
   (a) the foreign currency rises against the dollar
   (b) the foreign currency weakens against the dollar
   (c) it doesn't matter—you will pay the same no matter what

2. For most goods and services, if the price rises, consumer demand will:
   (a) rise
   (b) fall
   (c) stay the same
   (d) disappear because of price gouging

"Money often costs too much."
~ Ralph Waldo Emerson

3. A recession or depression is caused by:
   (a) people's fears about spending money
   (b) bank failures
   (c) crop failure
   (d) any or all of the above

4. When interest rates rise:

    (a) it costs more to refinance your mortgage

    (b) your retirement savings grow faster

    (c) it eventually costs more to buy almost anything

    (d) all of the above

Earning

5. When working to earn money, it's best to:

    (a) have more than one source of income in case one dries up

    (b) focus only on the job you have to do your best and earn your employer's loyalty

    (c) live below your means so that you don't have to touch your savings

    (d) (a) and (c)

6. Running your own business always brings in more money than working for an employer:

    (a) True

    (b) False

7. If you work for some other gift or incentive rather than money, it doesn't count as income:

    (a) True

    (b) False

8. If your son goes to university and wants to get a part-time job to help with expenses, you tell him:

    (a) absolutely not—he'll have to make do on his college savings

(b) to work as many hours as he can to help fund his own schooling

(c) help him review his class schedule and decide how many hours he can work without jeopardizing his grades

Saving

9. It's okay to spend what you make as long as you're getting raises every year:

    (a) True   (b) False

10. Having available room on your credit card is the same thing as having an emergency fund:

    (a) True   (b) False

11. When saving for distant goals, it's best to:

    (a) lock in some of the savings to get the best interest rate

    (b) keep all funds liquid to ensure that you can always get at them on a moment's notice

    (c) invest in penny stocks as they have the best chance for a huge return

12. You have retirement savings accounts at each of your last three employers. You should:

    (a) leave them alone to lower the risk that all the funds will decline

    (b) talk to a financial advisor about amalgamating them into a single fund that you control

    (c) go back to work for one of the employers so that you can keep contributing to one of the plans

Spending

13. When you get to the grocery store, you find that the 12-pack of toilet paper you were going to buy is on sale for $4.99. The 4-pack of the same brand is $2.19 but has an in-store manufacturer's coupon for 35 cents, that the store will double. Which is the best buy?

    (a) the 4-pack with the coupons

    (b) the 12-pack, because larger sizes are always less expensive per unit

    (c) they're both exactly the same

> "Don't tell me where your priorities are. Show me where you spend your money and I'll tell you what they are."
> ~James W. Frick

14. When buying a new television that is on sale in this week's store flyer, you should:

    (a) buy it quickly before they run out

    (b) take time to compare features and quality ratings to other similar models

    (c) ask the retailer for a better price

    (d) (b) and (c)

15. Sales prices are always a better deal than the regular price:

    (a) True   (b) False

16. You just received a $215 surprise check as a partial refund for overpaying your electric bill during the year. You should:

    (a) treat your family to dinner out

    (b) spend half of it on compact fluorescent light bulbs to save even more on your electric bill in the future and save the other half

    (c) buy your kids those game console games they've been begging for for months

Banking & Credit

17. Having multiple credit cards with high balances is the best way to improve your credit rating:

    (a) True   (b) False

18. When you hold funds in a bank account, you are actually losing money because of inflation:

    (a) True   (b) False

    (c) it depends on the current state of the economy and the terms of the deposit

19. If you get behind on your house payments, you can turn the keys over to the lender and be clear of the debt:

    (a) yes, and it's better for your credit than going into foreclosure

    (b) yes, especially if you have lots of equity in the house because the lender will cut you a check for the difference

    (c) rarely, and, if the lender sells the house for less than you owe on it, you can still be responsible for the difference

20. Keeping all your savings in one bank is the best strategy:

    (a) yes, because they will give better loyalty rates

    (b) no, because banks fail all the time, best to spread it out

    (c) keeping an amount up to the insured limit is fine but the rest should be spread out amongst financial institutions

Business

21. It's okay not to make a profit for the first five years of your business:

    (a) yes, you should invest everything back into the company

(b) no, to be a successful business model, the business has to be able to pay for its labor and that includes you

(c) it can be financially traumatic to lose out on retirement savings contributions for five years if the business can't pay you

(d) (b) and (c)

22. The best form of advertising for your business is:

(a) phone book ads

(b) radio spots on your local station

(c) social media

(d) word-of-mouth and reputation

23. When setting the prices of your product or service, you should:

(a) see what your competitors are charging and set a lower price

(b) base your prices on what it costs to produce the product or provide the service

(c) factor in both your cost of production and what the market is used to paying

(d) start with a price lower than your cost and then raise it when you start attracting customers

24. If your daughter wants to start a dog-sitting business, you:

(a) offer to pay her upfront expenses for her: flyers, leashes, dog brushes, etc.

(b) tell her that she has to save up enough money for the expenses out of her allowance

(c) offer to loan her the money for start-up expenses at a reasonable interest rate after you have reviewed her business plan

Taxes

25. It doesn't make sense to work lots of overtime because the increase in taxes withheld can be higher than the increase in income:

    (a) True   (b) False

26. The income tax that you owe is limited to the amount taken off your paychecks by your employer:

    (a) Yes, the employer is required to withhold the correct amount and she must make up any difference

    (b) No, your taxes are based on your individual financial situation and you may owe more taxes at the end of the year

    (c) You can ask your employer to take off extra taxes if you think you will owe at the end of the year.

    (d) both (a) and (c)

> "Money never starts an idea. It is always the idea that starts the money."
> ~ Owen Laughlin

27. A progressive tax system, such as that in Canada and the United States:

    (a) means that higher levels of income have a higher income tax rate

    (b) means that everyone pays the same amount of tax

    (c) means that taxpayers are responsible for calculating and remitting their own taxes

28. Which tax form tells your employer how much tax and other deductions to make on your paycheck?

    (a) a TD1 form in Canada and a W-4 form in the United States

    (b) a T1 in Canada and a 1040 in the United States

    (c) the employee's last income tax return in both countries

Insurance

29. Basic house insurance covers the following:

    (a) floods

    (b) hurricane damage

    (c) fire

    (d) mold damage

30. Life insurance covers you until your death as long as you keep paying premiums:

    (a) True   (b) False

31. Taking out life insurance on your children should be an important part of your insurance planning:

    (a) True   (b) False

32. The most important criteria to compare when looking for property insurance is:

    (a) claims-paying reputation

    (b) policy cost

    (c) length of time the company has been around

    (d) coverage inclusions

    (e) (a), (c), and (d)

Allowances

33. Kids as young as three can understand the connection between working and earning money:

    (a) True   (b) False

34. Teaching kids how to earn and manage an allowance:

    (a) gives them practice for handling their own money in the future

    (b) helps them learn that money is a scarce resource

    (c) shows them how to deal with non-financial decision-making

    (d) all of the above

35. Your son wants to buy a full-featured gaming laptop rather than the student computer you were planning to buy him, you will:

    (a) tell him he has to save up for the difference in price

    (b) buy him the basic computer anyway

    (c) tell him that he has to do without until his wants are more reasonable

    (d) buy him the more expensive computer

36. Kids should start saving for long-term goals, such as university and their first car as soon as they start to receive an allowance:

    (a) True   (b) False

Budgeting

37. Only adults need to keep detailed budgets:

    (a) True   (b) False

    (c) even adults don't need to keep a budget as long as they are saving some of their income

38. Emergency funds should be used in the following situations:

   (a) new windows for the house

   (b) unexpected dishwasher repairs

   (c) a hotel room following a house fire

   (d) emergency vet bills after your dog is hit by a car

   (e) (c) and (d)

39. Discretionary expenses include:

   (a) mortgage payments

   (b) groceries

   (c) car loan payments

   (d) electric bill

40. The first step in setting up a monthly budget is:

   (a) decide how much you want to put into savings every month

   (b) detail out current spending for 2-3 months

   (c) allocate any extra funds to paying down debt

   (d) find out how much other people spend on monthly expenses

"A penny saved is a penny earned."
~ Benjamin Franklin

Answers:

1:(a), 2:(b), 3:(d), 4:(d), 5:(d), 6:(b), 7:(b), 8:(c), 9:(b), 10:(b), 11:(a), 12:(b), 13:(a), 14:(d), 15:(b), 16:(b), 17:(b), 18:(c), 19:(c), 20:(c), 21:(d), 22:(d), 23:(c), 24:(c), 25:(b), 26:(d), 27:(a), 28:(a), 29:(c), 30:(b), 31:(b), 32:(e), 33:(a), 34:(d), 35:(a), 36:(a), 37:(b), 38:(e), 39:(b), 40:(b)

Score:

1-20:   Time to start some intensive financial rehabilitation

21-30:   You have the basics down but need some fiscal fine-tuning

31-40:   You have a great start at giving your kids a valuable monetary education

✓ SUMMARY

- Before you can help guide your children on their own money path, it's important to take a look at your own. What money myths are you still carrying around that can be dispelled with a little studying?

- The most basic foundation pillar of financial responsibility is to name every dollar. All incoming funds should already have a plan before they pass through your fingers (or your debit card).

- The words that you use to talk about money can affect the way your children perceive it. If you talk about finances like they are controlling you and not the other way around, it can convey to your kids that learning money management is useless. Use strong, confident terms when discussing how you are handling your finances.

- No one expects you to be a perfect fiscal manager. Everyone makes mistakes along the way and that's perfectly okay. Your kids learn from both your successes and your stumbles. Teaching your kids how to pick themselves up and dust themselves off when they make money mistakes is a valuable lesson.

- There are many books and courses that can help you brush up your own financial skills if those need some work.

DIANNE'S STORY

My kids opened bank accounts when they were 10 years old. Early on, they deposited their birthday money in there, with no real restrictions on it, as they learned to deposit money and use their debit card. As soon as they got a part-time job on a regular basis, we implemented the "mom and dad tax": 50 percent of all earnings go into a bank account set up for them, but they do not have access to it. They will get it back when they start their first year of post-secondary education. The 50 percent they get to keep, they can spend as they see fit. But they are required to pay for 1/2 of their post-secondary and for miscellaneous other things (school lunches, car insurance, etc.).

If I had to share more financial knowledge with my kids right now, I would tell them to think ahead, figure out a way to question whether they need or want something. Debt is something to avoid at all costs and credit card debt should NEVER happen.

At age 14, both started refereeing hockey in the winter and soccer in the summer. One babysits and one has had full-time summer jobs at 16 that continue part-time through the school year.

If our kids wanted to come back home and live with us as adults, we would not allow them to indefinitely, but would for a period of time. We would charge them room and board as long as the situation was such that they were working. If they were not working but trying earnestly to find work, I would not kick them out on the street.

I used inheritance money to set up an RESP for our kids' education, and have made contributions from household money. This will pay for approximately 1/2 of all costs—the rest they are responsible for. If they do not finish post-secondary education, they are required to pay the money back to me.

~ DIANNE B., WELLESLEY, ONTARIO

CHAPTER THREE

Supply & Demand: Economics for Kids

✓ INTRODUCTION

When you think about the term "economics," you may picture university students sitting in a classroom, listening to a droning old professor reading endlessly from a dusty textbook. It may seem like something that is best taught at that level for those who may need the information someday.

However, everyone needs to have a basic understanding of how the economy works to really grasp money and its role in our lives. Without knowing what impact certain world events are likely to have on our own country's monetary policy, we won't know whether our paycheck will buy us more or less next month or next year. Without knowing the economic risks we might face, it is impossible to brace for potential job loss or mortgage rate hikes. Economics affects us all.

That doesn't mean that you should run right out and buy some books by economists such as John Maynard Keynes or Adam Smith for your kids' bedtime reading pleasure. But kids can understand basic concepts like what exactly money is and how it circulates around from businesses to people to businesses.

✓ THE BIRTH OF AN ECONOMY

Trading goods with others has been around for over five thousand years. Surviving documents and tablets show the workings of Ebla, a thriving trading city excavated in what is Syria today. As early as 2250 BC, Ebla merchants were trading fabrics, dyes, and precious metals with Sumerians by cart and oxen. Even at that early date, the Eblians had a sophisticated system of money and pricing and even gave receipts to their trading partners.

> "Money and women are the most sought after and the least known about of any two things we have"
> ~ Will Rogers

Later, trading routes developed along the Tigris and Euphrates rivers, using the water to trade large amounts of goods. In the 1st century BC, the Roman Empire controlled much of Europe and the Middle East and controlled trade through much of its territories.

In the middle of the 19th century AD, trade became industrialized throughout much of Europe and the Americas and many countries began to formalize trading agreements with other countries. As transportation became more reliable and grew in size, exporting goods in bulk became possible.

One great way to help younger kids understand the basics of trade is through a game. Bring over three of your child's friends and have each one of them set up their own village. They can make a flag for their village and come up with a name. Assign each village a major export, such as cloth, spices, tea, bronze, wheat, or olive oil. Explain to them that the item they export cannot otherwise be made or acquired by the other villages. In order to obtain any of the other goods, each village must trade for it.

Some progressive communities today have developed barter networks to encourage community-based commerce. These barter transactions are still subject to tax even though no actual money changes hands.

Start the trading by allowing each village to try to do direct barters (e.g., I'll give you 20 gallons of olive oil for 3 pounds of tea). Give each child a piece of paper and pencil to help them work out their pricing systems. After a short amount of time, the villagers will likely discover that it can be difficult and confusing to have to come up with equivalents for each other's item, such as 1 foot of cloth equals 1 ounce of spices, a quart of wheat, and a pint of olive oil. They will notice that it is hard to keep each trade equivalent in value. They may also have a hard time trading for exactly what they want when they have to trade one-on-one. In economics, this concept is called the double-coincidence of wants. It means that, when people barter without common currency, they need to trade with people that have exactly what they want and who need exactly what they have.

Then, dispense beans! Give each village 100 dried beans. It doesn't matter what kind of beans. Have every village agree on the value of the beans, for example, a gallon of oil costs 25 beans, a bolt of cloth costs 37, etc. Once the value of the beans has been established, allow them to resume their trading and see how much easier it is with a common currency. This helps kids understand how monetary systems arose and why they are important to people's everyday life.

✓ WHAT IS MONEY?

"Money" can be a confusing concept for both children and adults to get our heads around. We think of money, in the most general sense, as something of value in its own right. However, money only has value because we say it does. It is not much more than a promise to pay—more like an IOU note. There was a time when established currencies like the dollar and the pound sterling were tied to actual wealth. They represented how much gold was owing to someone. Rather than hauling gold bars or a bag of gold coins out every time you wanted to buy some bread, governments stored gold and printed money to stand in its place, a much easier and lighter substitute.

The first metal coins came from China around 1000 B.C. as a replacement for the cowrie shells the Chinese had been using. These original coins were made of bronze and copper and often sported a hole so that they could be linked together on a chain.

Some gold and silver coins are still in existence today but are worth far more than their face value. For example, the Canadian Maple Leaf silver dollar and the U.S. Eagle silver dollar are both 1 ounce of almost pure silver, making them worth more than $35 at the time of this printing. Today's dollar coins are made from lighter and lower-value metals.

In the early 20th century, the governments of the United Kingdom, Canada, and the United States abandoned the link between physical gold deposits and money and began issuing notes with no backing. While this gave them more flexibility to increase the money supply artificially to lower interest rates, it has led to currency fluctuations and other economic imbalances.

There are several definitions of money, including deposits held in banks, notes and coins in people's pockets, and liquid term deposits. The value of that money to purchase goods and services depends on many economic factors that we will discuss a little later.

It's also important to define for kids what money isn't. It isn't a credit card or line of credit, although many people use these vehicles as substitutes for money. Money is wealth that is owed to us, not debt that is being extended to us.

> The economy depends about as much on economists as the weather does on weather forecasters.
> ~Jean-Paul Kauffmann

✓ CAN'T WE JUST PRINT MORE MONEY?

As kids learn more about how money circulates in the economy, an inevitable question arises: Why don't we just print more money if we don't have enough? It certainly sounds like a logical solution. If everyone has more money, then everyone is wealthier. Right?

As we have witnessed throughout history around the world, increasing a country's money supply serves to devalue the currency and cause rampant inflation. At its most basic, even if the amount of money everyone has rises, the amount of "stuff" in the world to buy does not. More dollars chase the same amount of goods. As demand for goods increases, so do the prices.

To show kids an example of this phenomenon, drag out your old Monopoly game the next time your child's friends are over. Let's say there are five children. Bring out a plate of four cookies and place them in front of the kids. Dole out a Monopoly hundred dollar bill to each child as their salary. Give two of the children an extra hundred dollar bill each because they earn more money at their jobs. Tell the kids that you are selling the cookies for $125 each. The two who earned more will likely hand you the money and eat their cookie, while the three who didn't earn enough will sit there and glare. Replace the two cookies on the plate. Now hand out $1,000 to each child and tell them that the cookies are still $125. Each of the five will likely try to pay you for one but you only have four. Because the demand exceeds the supply, one or more of the children will try to offer you more than $125, starting a bidding war. As the price begins to approach $1,000, one or more may hesitate but at least one will be willing to hand over all $1,000 for a cookie. The price of the cookies is now what the market will bear—$1,000, an 800 percent increase in price. The fact that everyone now makes $1,000 in salary is offset by the fact that a cookie now costs $1,000. The increase in the money supply has caused rampant inflation. You may be asked: Why don't you just make more cookies? This also seems like a reasonable solution. Try to hire one of the children to make the cookies for $100 (in Monopoly money, of course) and see if they are willing to do that. Now that they have $1,000 in their hands, they are less likely to work for the same wage as before. You'll have to offer more. The higher the wages, the more expensive the cookies have to be. There is no way to keep prices down when the money supply increases.

I have young boys ages 10, 5, and 2. They understand that when I say, "No, we cannot afford it," it means that we need to save our money for more important things. My ten-year-old understands that we are middle class, not rich, not poor, but that we work hard for everything that we have. My five- and two-year-old sons do not understand our financial situation, but are starting to understand the concept of money.

~ AMANDA H., PHILADELPHIA, PENNSYLVANIA

✓ HOW GOODS & SERVICES TRADE HANDS- MICROECONOMICS

Microeconomics is the study of how individuals, groups, and businesses make financial decisions and how those decisions affect others. It looks at how we decide to spend our income, what decisions we would make if our income changed, and how we determine relative value. All of these things affect our everyday life as we spend and save and budget.

One major microeconomic concept is opportunity cost. Understanding opportunity costs helps us to come to decisions about how we spend money. Money is a scarce resource (i.e., it doesn't really grow on trees) and we have to make choices about what to give it up for. As adults, we have to decide between putting it in the bank or spending it on a vacation. We have to choose between buying a Ford or a Toyota. For kids, these decisions may include choosing between spending money now on a DVD or saving it up to buy an mp3 player. While the decisions are of a smaller magnitude, the tools we use to evaluate which is the best option for us are the same. Opportunity cost forces us to look at what the next best use of the money is when we consider how much something really costs.

Let's look at an example. You can choose to take a year-long full-time certification course for $3,000. You estimate that having the course under your belt will allow you to make an extra $75,000 over the course of the next 10 years. At first glance, it seems like you are expending a total of $3,000 to get a benefit of $75,000— a no-brainer. However, let's look at what you would have been doing if you weren't taking the course: working full-time for your salary of $33,000. You are giving up that salary for a year to take the course, so the real cost is $3,000 plus $33,000 for a total of $36,000. It's still much less than the aggregate benefit you will get over the next decade and, in this case, probably still a good deal. If you don't look at the opportunity costs of your spending decisions, you are likely to seriously underestimate them.

To help kids understand the true costs of their decisions, walk through some of those decisions with them. Ask them what they would be doing with their money if they weren't using it for their chosen purpose. Get them to evaluate whether giving up the next choice activity or purpose is worth it to spend their money on their chosen item.

> "Money will come when you are doing the right thing."
> ~ Mike Phillips

Opportunity costs don't have to be solely financial. For example, if your daughter chooses to go out to a movie with her friends, she may lose out on the enjoyment of playing games on the computer at home. The value of these "soft" opportunity costs are harder to evaluate than monetary ones, but are just as important to take into consideration.

Another important microeconomic concept is supply and demand, and this is one that will affect many of your kids' buying decisions. Supply is the amount of goods or services a seller is willing to offer. Sellers want to get the best prices for their items and will, in most cases, offer more items the higher the price is. Demand is how much of those goods and services buyers are willing to purchase. For most goods, demand goes up (i.e., buyers want more) when the price goes down. This puts sellers and buyers at cross-purposes, the former looking for high prices and the latter looking for low ones. The price at which sellers are willing to offer the exact amount that buyers want to buy is called equilibrium. It is basically how prices are settled in a perfect free market economy. It doesn't always work so perfectly, especially when there are government restrictions placed on certain industries, but it works reasonably well the rest of the time.

So, how does this affect your life and that of your kids? Think about new-release movies. When a popular movie premieres in a theater, demand is very high. Many movie-goers want to see new movies the minute they are released. Because movie theaters know that they will have no problem selling tickets, most theaters do not offer any discounts or reduced prices on opening night. They can charge full price because they know they can fill the seats since the demand is there. After the movie has been in theaters for a few weeks, demand starts to taper off and the theater will start offering lower-priced tickets to stimulate demand. People who might not have paid the full $15 for a ticket on opening night might be more willing to pay $8 on a week night. After the movie is no longer in theaters, it will come out on DVD or Blu-ray and people can purchase it to watch as many times as they want. The DVD or Blu-ray will sell at a price that stimulates demand for those who want to watch the movie at home. Those who want to watch the newest movies always pay the most.

> The only reason a great many American families don't own an elephant is that they have never been offered an elephant for a dollar down and easy weekly payments.
> ~Mad Magazine

The same is true when purchasing this year's hot new toy at Christmas or buying current-season fashions. The higher the demand, the higher the price.

When talking to your kids about purchase decisions you are making or when you are helping them to make theirs, remind them that, often, when something is new and hot (and, therefore, in high demand), the price will often be higher than it will be a few months down the road. Help them to look at whether that difference in price is worth it to them to have the game or toy or dress right away when they could have the same thing in a little while and keep some money in their pockets.

In our house, my kids see me make those kinds of choices all the time. It's why I buy wrapping paper the day after Christmas for the next year and why I buy turkey for 39 cents a pound the day after Thanksgiving.

✓ HOW COUNTRIES TRADE WITH EACH OTHER–MACROECONOMICS

Macroeconomics is often a more difficult topic for kids to grasp than microeconomics. Looking at the larger picture of trade and commerce is less tangible to most kids (and lots of adults). However, your kids are inundated with talking-head sound bytes on television and newspaper headlines about the state of the economy every day. In recessionary times, they absorb news of the jobless rate increasing and they are likely to have friends whose parents have lost their jobs. Even if difficult economic times have not yet hit your family, your kids may be concerned that they will. They may not be able to articulate their fears or questions, but some basic understanding of the way the economy works can help them see that the economy goes through cyclical ups and downs and that it is a normal part of life. Not only may it ease some of their concerns but it will help them as adults to insulate themselves from the risk of recession.

The first thing to understand about macroeconomics is that there are many theories out there. These theories try to explain the connections between the value of money, interest rates, aggregate consumer demand, employment rates, and inflation. Economists are divided up into several camps on how these things affect the others and how best to stop economic cycles.

The good thing is that you don't need to delve into economic theory to help your kids understand the basics.

Start by asking your kids what they know about the economy. What are they hearing in the news about it? Pull out a newspaper and look at the headlines with them. Look at articles about jobs or the real estate market or inflation. Peruse the local section of the newspaper with your kids. Are stores closing in your town? Are new industries moving in? All of these stories are connected to what's happening at the national level.

Talk to your kids about economic cycles in ways that mean something tangible to them. For example, if your kids love lobster (or salmon or any other food that is considered a luxury), explain to them that, if you got a new high-paying job, they would probably get to eat lobster more often. If lots of people became employed

The Euro (€) is one of the world's newest currencies, beginning circulation in 2002. It is the official currency of 17 European countries, collectively called the Eurozone. It is the second largest reserve currency in the world after the U.S. dollar and is used daily by approximately 332 million Europeans.

because there were more jobs in the economy, the overall demand for lobster would go up and the stores selling it would earn more revenue. They would have to hire more people to sell the lobsters, creating more employment. They would also be ordering more lobster from the seafood company, who would have to hire more fishermen to catch lobsters. All of these new jobs would allow people to buy other things that they couldn't when they didn't have jobs, which increases incomes in other parts of the economy. It's an upward cycle. But, as we saw with the supply and demand equation on the microeconomic side, increased demand increases prices, which encourages inflation. Inflation will start to cool off demand once it gets too high. So, once lobsters are more expensive than they were before there was so much demand for them, the demand will slow, because people's incomes from their new jobs won't pay for as much anymore.

This self-regulating cycle causes the "waves" we see in the country's economy. It heats up, then cools off, then begins to heat up again, always working toward attaining equilibrium. (For economic geeks like me, this is part of Adam Smith's "invisible hand" concept.)

> The safe way to double your money is to fold it over once and put it in your pocket.
> ~Frank Hubbard

Sometimes, if the economy is getting hot or cold too fast, the government steps in to try to influence it back to a more stable position, just like if you saw your child swinging so high on a swing that she could fall off, you would slow the swing down. Whether and when the government should do this is the subject of much political debate. When we look back in recent history, there are times that government intervention in the economy made things worse instead of better.

The government has two main tools at its disposal and neither is the perfect one for the job. The first is the money supply. The government, through central banks, can cut back the total supply of money in an inflationary economy. The theory is that this will increase interest rates and slow down growth, reducing inflation. In a recession, the government can increase the supply of money to lower interest rates and encourage businesses to grow and consumers to spend.

The government can also influence interest rates more directly. The central bank (Bank of Canada in Canada or the Federal Reserve in the U.S.) lends money to the rest of the country's banks. If the central bank lowers the rate it lends to other banks, those banks lower the rates they charge borrowers and vice versa.

Talk to your kids about economic concepts in basic ways, using what they already hear and see in the media. This will help them learn how the wider economy affects them every day and how they can protect themselves from economic cycles when they become adults.

✓ WHAT CAUSES A RECESSION OR DEPRESSION?

The words "recession" and "depression" have been thrown around in the media and around water coolers since 2008. Both Canada and the United States experienced fallout from economic downturn (as did much of the rest of the world), but the U.S. was hit much harder due to the real estate market collapse.

The words may be frightening to children who are old enough to know that the Great Depression was a very bad thing, but who are too young to understand all of the economic nuances of the current financial crisis.

Economists and politicians can't agree on the exact causes of recession or depression (which is simply a deeper recession). They can't even agree on the official definition, which continues to change and evolve. While most economists agree that, as of 2011, both countries were out of danger of a recession, there are still concerns about economic growth going forward.

At its most basic, a recession is an economic cycle where businesses are producing less and jobs are drying up for an extended period of time. If we go back to the swing analogy above, sometimes the swing goes faster and sometimes slower, and it cycles between these speeds. A recession happens when the swing has slowed to the point where it's stalled and the rider can't kick her feet hard enough to get it going again. Some kind of outside force will have to come along and get the swing in motion again.

Not all of the recipe ingredients that go into baking a recession are strictly financial. How people feel about money also has a huge impact. For example, if you still had a job and believed that we were almost out of recession, you would make different spending choices than if the recession appeared as if it were going to continue indefinitely. In the first scenario, you might take your annual vacation to Key West. In the second, you might save that money instead, in case you need it to weather the continuing storm. How people perceive economic events changes their spending patterns, which affects business and investing. A widespread negative view of the country's financial future can actually prolong the recession and become a self-fulfilling prophecy.

Don't be afraid to talk to your children about these issues. It is impossible to shelter them from current economic events the moment they play with friends, go to school, or turn on television. Talk to them only to the point they have questions and can comprehend the answers. There's no need to bombard them with economic theory. Help them relate the basics of the economy to what they see in their day-to-day life. For example, if they have a friend whose mom lost her job through lay-off, you can explain how many businesses have to cut their expenses, such as employees, because they're not selling as much because the economy is slow. Or, if their favorite video store closes, talk to them about how people have less money to spend on entertainment and other discretionary items, so the store can't keep operating. Your goal is to shed some light on the inter-connections between your pocketbook and the national financial picture without introducing more fear about the future. Remind your children that the country has been through these cycles before and has emerged back out of them. Although no one can determine when the downturn will end, it definitely will end.

> "Money is usually attracted, not pursued."
> ~ Jim Rohn

✓ HOW GOOD MONEY SKILLS CAN LESSEN THE IMPACT OF FINANCIAL DOWNTURNS

Teaching your kids how to handle money wisely can help to protect them from the impact of recessions or other financial crises in the future, whether they are global, national, or even personal financial events.

The most important skill in surviving a recession is debt management. This should start well before the crisis hits. The more exposure to debt people have, the more vulnerable they will be if they lose their job or if interest rates go up.

Living below one's means is an old phrase but one that is still just as relevant today. Spending less than you bring in and saving the rest gives you a safety margin to wait out a financial hardship. When we talk about savings in detail in Chapter Five, "The Penny Jar: Teaching Kids About Saving," we'll look at the "savings buckets" and the importance of setting up an emergency fund.

At one time, I thought revealing all of that information to children was a very bad idea. My parents actually kept that stuff secret when I was smaller and I wish they had not. It kind of hit me like a ton of bricks when I suddenly realized that I was responsible for myself at 18. If I had known more, I would certainly have been better prepared. We try to strike a balance with our nine-year-old twin daughters. We tell them what it means to pay bills and be responsible, but we do not go into details that would concern them at such a young age.

~ RODNEY S., GREENSBORO, NORTH CAROLINA

✓ SUMMARY

- Money developed as a common trading medium that made buying and selling transactions easier and more consistent. Money has been around in one form or another for more than four thousand years.

- Microeconomics is the study of how consumers interact with businesses and other consumers. It shows us how the demand and supply for products changes as prices go up and down.

- Macroeconomics is the study of how economies interact with one another. It looks at the impact that interest rates, foreign exchange rates, and trade deficits have on each other and it explains concepts like inflation and recession.

- A recession or depression can have many causes, not all of which are financial. Consumers' confidence in the future of the economy can have a large impact on what happens in the economy.

- A solid financial education can help cushion you from economic downturns by helping you understand how to protect your own wealth and reduce your financial risks.

SAMANTHA'S STORY

My kids don't receive an allowance. With my oldest being only four, their concept of money isn't all that great. Their "earning" system is set up through sticker charts and the ability to earn rewards with certain amounts of stickers.

My best advice to my kids as they become adults will be "Don't be wasteful." As an example, figure out what you need for school, then take out $1,000 more than that and set it aside. Emergencies come up. Supplies are needed. Things happen. Don't waste the $1,000 on stupid things. If it's still there at the end of the semester, leave it there or pay it back toward your loans and debt.

Right now, my children are much too young to understand finances, but they do know that sometimes mommy and daddy have to say no because we don't have the money for something. Our oldest has become more curious about money and has asked more questions. She is beginning to understand some of it, and I have, on occasion, allowed her to "pay" for things (handing my money to the cashier) to help her understand the connection between payment and receipt of products.

I don't know if I would let my kids live with me as adults. It would depend on the situation. If my child truly needed to live with me (unplanned pregnancy, divorce, illness), I doubt I would charge room and board. If they wanted to live with me due to circumstances within their control (laziness, not earning enough, etc.) then I might charge some. If they were in college, I might waive any kind of rent as well, as long as they maintained good grades. They would, however, regardless of why they are living with me, be required to contribute toward the household by keeping things clean, doing chores, helping cook, etc.

I would like to help my children with college costs, but it really depends. In our current situation, we couldn't afford to pay for any of these expenses. I am enrolled with the University of Alaska and am pursuing my bachelor's degree in biological sciences in hopes of getting into medical school one day. I hope that when the time comes, I will be able to help my children with school, but we won't know until we're there. Even if I am able to help financially, there will be rules. I will pay for classes up front; however, their grades will determine how much they will owe me when the semester is over. If they get an A, I will pay for the course. If they get a B, they will owe me half of the cost of that course, and if they get a C, they are responsible for the entire cost.

~ SAMANTHA V., SOLDOTNA, ALASKA

CHAPTER FOUR

Pay Day: Teaching Kids About Earning Money

✓ INTRODUCTION

When my daughter was six years old, she asked me, "How come the mailman gives you money?" It took me a moment to puzzle through her question. As far as I knew, the mailman had not given me anything but my mail in all the years I had known him. No flowers, no gifts, and certainly not any money. After a moment, I realized that she was talking about my income. Most of my income comes by way of checks through the mail. Even though my daughter and her brother are well-versed in money matters, misconceptions still arise.

How much do your kids know about where your income comes from? Do they know what you bring home every week or two? In order for them to truly understand the need for saving and wise spending, they must understand where money comes from and why it is a scarce commodity.

You may be afraid that, if you tell your children how much you make, the entire town will know. Have a discussion with your children about discretion. Let them know it's okay to talk about the specifics of your family's financial situation at home, but not with friends, teachers, or other people in the community. It's not safe to discuss money matters widely, just like it's not safe to let everyone know that you just bought a new flat-screen television. Also, explain that talking about money with friends can make some kids feel bad or anxious about their own family's financial situation.

✓ THE NEED TO EARN

Many kids under 10 do not naturally make a direct connection between their parents' going off to work every day and having enough money for household expenses. Because most types of pay are now given by check or by direct deposit into a bank account, it's easy even for adults to sometimes lose the connection.

Find out what your kids know about what you do for a living. Do they know how you get paid (by the hour, salary, or commission)? Do they understand how you got your job or started your business? Earning money is the first step in financial security and kids need a basic understanding of how money comes in the door in the first place.

Older kids may have more philosophical questions for you, such as why you do the kind of work you do. The discussion may start to move toward career choices, but the basic principle of the conversation should be that people work to earn money to live.

✓ WHY DON'T KIDS HAVE JOBS?

If earning money is such an important thing, why don't kids work, too? When my son was eight, he decided that he was going to go straight to working and skip all of the boring school years. His motivation was two-fold: first, he thought that going off to work every day was far cooler than sitting in a classroom learning math and history. The second was his reasoning that the sooner he started earning income, the richer he would be as an adult. It was a long-thought-out, if faulty, plan.

I asked him what it was he was going to do for money. At the time, he was obsessed with J.K. Rowling's Harry Potter series of books. "I want to be a wizard," he said. I asked him what he knew about being a wizard. "Not much," he said, "but I can learn on the job." I reminded him gently that even Harry Potter had to go to school to become a wizard. There were simply no entry-level wizard jobs to be had. Although deflated, he grudgingly admitted that he might have to stay in school longer.

> They who are of the opinion that Money will do everything, may very well be suspected to do everything for Money.
> ~George Savile,
> Complete Works, 1912

Teaching kids about earning income should include a discussion about the benefits of staying in school and potentially deferring jumping into the working or business world. Explain that going to school—whether elementary, secondary, or university—is an investment in future earnings. Just the same way as you put away savings now to allow them to grow over time, the more education children get, the more likely it is that they will have a higher earnings potential down the road. Most well-paying jobs require a university or college degree right off the bat, and many require even further certification and training. Spending the time and money to develop an education pays off in higher paychecks down the road. The same is true for business owners. The more an entrepreneur learns about commerce, accounting, marketing, and human resources, the more likely she will be to succeed.

My daughter is nine years old and has wanted to get a "real job" since she was six. She feels like working every day is where all the fun is and that school gets in the way of that. I have to keep telling her that there are exciting and fulfilling jobs and there are hard and boring jobs. Staying in school increases the chances she will have the job she wants some day. There are lots of ways to earn a living and I want to make sure she has the best chance of making lots of money doing what she loves to do—whatever that may be in the future.

~ LARA V., MONTREAL, QUEBEC

✓ SOURCES OF INCOME

People make money in many different ways and each family has its own combination of financial inputs into its household budget. You may run your own business and your spouse works for an employer. Or most of your income may come from investments. Explain to your children where your money comes from and how it is earned. It's important for kids to understand that earning income from any source takes work, skill, and effort. Income is never guaranteed and it is sometimes necessary or desirable to change your source of income. My kids have seen this first-hand in our home as I went from working for a large corporation to running my own accounting and consulting practice to writing full-time. The income stream looked different at every stage but it all contributed to the household budget.

> We can tell our values by looking at our checkbook stubs.
> ~Gloria Steinem

✓ EMPLOYMENT

When you work for someone else, you agree to trade your time and labor for payment. You don't own the business you work for, nor do you take any of the risks of loss (except for the potential loss of your job). Employees earn a fixed rate of money based on their role or the time they put in. Payment for services can be a fixed salary, an hourly wage, or even based on sales or other performance indicators.

Kids can relate employment income to their allowances—they're given a fixed amount of money for doing a certain job. If they do it, they get paid. If not, they don't get the money. Just like employees, kids are expected to do their "jobs" to a standard that you, the employer, sets. They are not free to do the work however they want or to hire others to do it for them. Unlike working for themselves, they can be "fired" from their chores if they do a bad job and then they won't get paid.

The word "salary" comes from the Latin word for salt, salarium. Roman soldiers were paid for their services in salt as it was a critical commodity. To remain in active service, soldiers had to earn their salary or be "worth their salt."

Not everyone who is terminated from their job was let go because they did a bad job, and this is an important concept for children to understand. It is likely that your child knows a friend or acquaintance who has a parent who has lost a job. It could have been through widespread layoffs or changes in staffing levels. Employees, unlike business owners, face the risk of losing their job and income source at any point in time.

If someone in your family works for an employer, show your kids the paycheck or pay stub and explain how the gross amount is calculated. For example, you may have worked for 43.5 hours at $18.25 an hour for a total of $793.88 gross. Then show them all of the deductions that come off until you get down to the net pay, which is what you get to take home. We'll talk more about taxes in Chapter Nine, "A Little Off the Top: All About the Taxman."

✓ COMMISSIONED SALES

> It is an unfortunate human failing that a full pocketbook often groans more loudly than an empty stomach.
> ~Franklin Delano Roosevelt

A commissioned salesperson is, in effect, halfway between an employee and a business owner, but most often is treated as an employee for tax purposes. A commissioned salesperson still earns money from an employer but the income is based on the amount of product or services the individual sells. Therefore, the employee is responsible for the amount of income she earns.

One way to show younger children how this works is to have them participate in a commission situation. Offer them 25 cents for every dandelion they pull in the backyard. If you run a business, you can "hire" your children to sell your products or services at a business expo or in your store (under your supervision, of course). They will have to act like a business owner to pitch the products or services but will be paid a fixed amount per sale from you.

✓ BUSINESS

Kids love businesses and most of them are budding entrepreneurs! In Chapter Eight, "Lessons of the Lemonade Stand: Business Principles for Kids," we will look at business principles in more depth, but begin by explaining that owning a business is another way to earn money.

The main differences between being a business owner and working at a job are risk and reward. Business owners take on all the risks of the enterprise. If the business fails, the owner can be personally responsible for paying the debts of the business. If the business doesn't make money, it's the owners, not the employees, who don't get paid. The owner can also be sued in business for many things, including negligence and breach of contract. An employee is sheltered from most of these business realities. Although employees run the risk of losing their job and their source of income if something goes wrong in the business, they are not on the hook for further losses.

At the other end of the spectrum, business owners also stand to gain from the enterprise if it does well. An owner takes all of the net profits. She can invest them back into the business or use them in any way she sees fit. Potentially, the profits from a business are unlimited. This is the reason that business owners are willing to take the risks—so that they may be able to reap the rewards. On the other hand, an employee simply trades their labor for a fixed amount of money.

Owning your own business also allows you to set up and operate a company the way you want to, not the way someone tells you to. A business owner has the flexibility to change the direction of the company or any of its procedures in order to attract more customers or make more money. An employee does not have this freedom (although, as I tell my consulting clients, smart business owners will solicit input from their employees).

My youngest son just got his first bank account. He is 17. He had to have a job and he has to save 10 percent of each paycheck into his savings account. He also has to give me $50 per month toward groceries. The rest is his to spend but I won't lend him money if he spends unwisely. He must buy his own jeans and tee-shirts (except for gifts) and he must pay his own car insurance and anything else he wants.

~ LINDA K., CHEWELAH, WASHINGTON

✓ INVESTMENT INCOME

Chapter Seven, "Piggy Banks & Plastic: Teaching Kids About Banking and Credit," discusses investing money in more detail. Some people, especially in retirement, are able to live partly or totally from the investment income they have made over time on their savings.

Once your kids begin to save and invest their own money, they will understand that their savings are growing not just because they keep putting more money in, but also because that money is earning income, whether it is interest, dividends, or capital gains. Even though the investment income may seem small in the beginning, it will grow substantially over time.

Investment income is considered passive income, whereas employment and business income is active. Passive income doesn't require continual effort and labor to get it. It grows on its own, with occasional review and reshuffling of investments. It is a great way to make more money while you are already earning active income. You can't work two jobs at the exact same time but you can have a job and earn investment income at the same time. It's a way of making your money work for you rather than you having to work for your money.

To show your kids how investment income can add up over time, show them an example of the benefits of compound interest. You can have your children take out pencil, paper, and calculator and work it out for themselves (my recommended method) or simply give them the facts. Start by asking them how much money they think they would have if they invested $10 a month at 5 percent interest for 20 years. You may get a wide variety of answers. After all, $10 per month doesn't seem like a lot of money. The total amount contributed is $2,400 over the 20 years. The total value of the investment, however, is $4,110.34. In other words, your child would have total investment income of $1,710.34.

If you want them to calculate the income themselves, you can have them "cheat" and use the future value of an annuity function on a scientific calculator or do it the old-fashioned way. I recommend that kids learn all of their math first by hand before they start using short cuts. This type of math is suitable for most kids over 10. Have them work out the interest earned in the first year as an example.

The first calculation is to turn the 5 percent annual rate into a monthly rate because we are adding new funds every month. 5 percent divided by 12 months is .42 percent (to keep it to two decimals and make it slightly easier). The first year of the investment is 12 periods, representing months. Have your child write 1 to 12 in a column. Then, make a column for contributions, investment totals, interest rate, and interest for the period. The investment total for each month is the sum of the investment total for the previous month, the interest for the previous month, and the current month's contributions. Here's an example:

Period	Contribution	Total	Interest Rate	Interest for period
1	10.00	10.00	.42	.04
2	10.00	20.04	.42	.08
3	10.00	30.08	.42	.13
4	10.00	40.21	.42	.17
5	10.00	50.38	.42	.21
6	10.00	60.59	.42	.25
7	10.00	70.84	.42	.30
8	10.00	81.14	.42	.34
9	10.00	91.48	.42	.38
10	10.00	101.86	.42	.43
11	10.00	112.29	.42	.47
12	10.00	122.76	.42	.52
Totals	120.00			3.32

As your kids will see, they have earned a total of $3.32 in income in the first year on their monthly contributions of $10.

My son has his first job this year. He works part-time at Home Depot as a Sales Associate. He is very proud of the job and takes his work very seriously. He spent two weeks in training, learning all there is to know about the garden area — which pesticides are effective for which pests, what time of year certain bugs come out, how to diagnose the most common issues with lawn mowers and tractors, and so forth. He really enjoys working and working with people. He comes home after work every day tired, but happy and satisfied. We insisted that half of his earnings are put into a savings account so that he'll have some spending money during the winter at college. The other half he spends. Since we are driving him to and from work, we charge him a nominal gas fee to begin teaching him about regular expenses and planning his cash flow.

~ BRAD S., STRAFFORD, NEW HAMPSHIRE

✓ INTRODUCING YOUR KIDS TO EARNING MONEY

There are many ways to get your kids started earning money other than through allowance. In Chapter Eight, we'll look at business ideas for kids who have an entrepreneurial urge. There are other ways, however, that you can start your kids on the earning path.

My son and daughter first started earning money in yard sales. Every summer, we would gather together all of the clutter we had accumulated, and the things we no longer needed or had outgrown, and set up a yard sale. The kids would help me make the signs, set the prices, and set up the tables. During the sale itself, they were responsible for selling their own toys and books that they no longer wanted. They had their own cash boxes and handled their own money. After the sale, they were allowed to spend that money on anything they liked. It was both a great way to de-clutter the house and to give the kids first-hand experience with bringing in money.

Other ideas include letting your kids set up and run a bake sale or offer to work for friends or neighbors after school for money if it is age appropriate.

I pay my kids to do chores around the house. They need to have some sort of income and I'd rather pay them than someone else. Also, I'm not comfortable with them going out and working at a job. I'm not convinced they will be properly supervised and protected. If I put them to work, I know how well they can follow instructions and how well they can perform the job. It gives them the money they need and gives me the help that I need— a win/win situation.

~ MIA C., SELKIRK, MANITOBA

✓ SUMMARY

- Young children often don't make a natural connection between their parents' going off to work in the morning and being able to bring home groceries in the evening. Talk to your kids about how your family makes its money.

- Families can have one of several different sources of income or a combination of them. Kids should learn the basic differences between the employer/employee relationship and the entrepreneur/customer one.

- Income can be active or passive. Active income, such as employment income, requires continuous time and effort to create. Passive income, such as investment income, happens without continuous effort. Business income can be either active or passive, depending on the role of the owner in the business.

- It's important for kids to see the trade-offs of staying in school versus working for a living. The time spent in school is an investment that is likely to pay off with a more fulfilling and better-paying job down the road.

- Kids can get hands-on experience with earning income at a young age, both through entrepreneurial pursuits like setting up a lemonade stand, or through managing their own investment income.

BONNIE'S STORY

Looking back, I wish I would have shown my kids the importance of putting money away for retirement. Even a small amount each week would have been worth it.

My kids got savings accounts through school. The bank put in $5.00. There were no debit cards then. The kids were supposed to save some, but they pretty well did what they wanted with the accounts.

My advice for my kids is that they really need to know that, when they get a loan, they will have to pay it back, so be as frugal as possible and start the payback as soon as you can. Plan your money for the year and stick to it.

I never shared my personal financial information with my kids. At that time in my life, I didn't feel it was their business. Actually, I guess I still feel that way.

My children had to work if they wanted extra money for things that I couldn't afford to buy. They had paper routes and babysat.

To help them over a rough time, my kids would have to pay room and board if they wanted to come back home to live. I probably would save some to help them get their own place again. I enjoy my time without a lot of people around all the time so I would not encourage a long stay.

Day-to-day things they could buy whenever they wanted, but if they wanted to go to, say, Disneyland or something, they would have to save some toward it. Large items needed to be discussed as I didn't believe in how many families do things nowadays. We had one TV, not one in every room.

~ BONNIE H., STRATFORD, ONTARIO

CHAPTER FIVE

The Penny Jar: Teaching Kids About Saving Money

✓ INTRODUCTION

When I was a little girl, I had a parade of piggy banks. Some of them had been peanut butter jar bears and some were traditional porcelain pigs. Several played a little tune when you slid a coin in the slot and one said "thank you" in a slightly frightening monotone voice every time you fed it.

The very first piggy bank that I remember was also my favorite. It was a cat, rather than a pig, handcrafted in pine in an exaggerated abstract shape. Its main feature was its open sides; large round holes covered by thin Plexiglas. It didn't make any noise when I dropped coins inside but I could see them when they went in. I could see how my savings were growing slowly over time with every nickel or dollar bill I put in there. I loved to sit cross-legged on my bed after school and look at the growing collection of coins and bills and even an English pound that some relative had brought me back from a trip.

Being able to physically see my money grow helped make saving money real to me in a way a number in a bank book never could. When I got older, I did trade in my piggy banks for bank accounts, but, by then, I had the savings habit ingrained.

✓ HELPING YOUNG KIDS "SEE" THEIR SAVINGS

> There is a very easy way to return from a casino with a small fortune: go there with a large one.
> ~Jack Yelton

There are many ways to get your kids started on the path to learning good saving habits, but none is as effective and simple as starting them out with a piggy bank or even just a jar. Kids can begin to grasp basic money concepts almost as soon as they can walk and it's never too early to let them start accumulating some coins.

Young kids can add to their savings in many ways: from their chores (see Chapter 11), from gifts from family, and even from scrounging in couch cushions. There is no such thing as "not enough money to bother with." Help kids understand that every penny counts—literally. Allow them to pick up pennies on the sidewalk and add them to their savings. That way, they learn that all money is to be respected and cared for. People who don't learn to care for the pennies when they're young grow into adults who waste dollar bills…and ten-dollar bills.

The U.S. penny costs 1.79 cents each to produce due to high metal costs. It is made from 97.5 percent zinc and 2.5 percent copper.

Let kids count their stash as often as they like. Schools often teach coin recognition in the second and third grade when they start to teach the concept of fractions, but there's no need to wait that long. Kids can learn that four quarters make a dollar and that two dimes and a nickel are the same thing as a quarter before they start kindergarten.

As soon as kids are old enough to count their money, tape a piece of paper on the outside of the jar and let them update their balance every time they count. This gives them a second way to see that their money is growing. There are (expensive) piggy banks on the market today that use coin recognition technology and keep a running balance but nothing beats a canning jar, a pencil and paper, and some basic math skills.

My children are given money weekly to learn about money management and tithing. They do not earn this money for doing chores. Chores are the work that families do together because they love one another. We do not pay them for being a part of the family. They do have the option to earn money, though, by doing things above and beyond normal work from time to time.

My oldest is 8 years old and we just opened him a savings account to learn about saving money.

I need to talk to my children more about the folly of debt. Paying interest to borrow money is never a good idea. If the money is not in your pocket or your account, you should not spend it.

~ JACOB W., GLADSTONE, MISSOURI

✓ THE SAVINGS BUCKETS

> Inflation is when you pay fifteen dollars for the ten-dollar haircut you used to get for five dollars when you had hair.
> ~Sam Ewing

Once kids have the basic saving habit down pat, they are ready to learn about having different savings goals, just like grown-ups. Some savings goals are short term, like pizza and a movie, and some are longer term, such as a new bike or game console. The longest savings goals can be several years in the future, like saving for a first car or for university.

Having separate savings goals helps kids to analyze what the most important use of money is to them. They learn that if they don't buy Pokemon cards for three weeks, they can instead buy a DVD of their favorite movie. This is the first step toward understanding the scarcity of money. There will never be enough money for everything a child wants, just like in the grown-up world.

The savings "buckets" are simply the various savings goals. With younger children still working with piggy banks or jars, it means that they will have more of them. There may be a jar for weekly spending money, another for video games, and a third that represents saving for university. The kids will have to decide how to split money they get amongst the savings buckets.

✓ HELPING KIDS SPLIT THEIR MONEY BETWEEN BUCKETS

This is where you come in as a parent or teacher. Kids need to be in the lead in making their decisions about how much of their saved money goes into each bucket, but you can help guide them. Talk to your kids about their various goals and help them do the math to figure out how long it will take to get there. For example, if your daughter wants to save up for a Kindle, help her work out how long that will take if she funds it with $1 a week of her savings or with $2. Help her understand that the more money that goes in, the sooner she will meet her goal. She may decide that she's willing to give up buying smaller things in order to bolster her savings buckets for larger items.

Another way to make savings goals more visual to small children is to have them cut out a picture of what they're saving for and tape it to the outside of the jar. It's a tangible reminder of the purpose of tucking the money away. You can even have your child write the total amount needed to be saved and a goal date so that she can see progress.

✓ SETTING SAVINGS GOALS

The first step in setting savings goals with your kids is deciding what they are going to be responsible for buying. Will you pay for a new bike every year or are your kids responsible for that? Will they participate in saving for college or will you fund that for them? Kids need to know this kind of information in order to make reasonable savings goals.

Once kids are clear on what they need to save for, they can make more informed choices. The easiest way to get kids to save without a fight is to set ground rules with them. For example, the rule could be that every time your child comes into money, at least 10 percent goes to the college fund and 40 percent goes to other long-term savings. The rest can be spent or saved as the child chooses. This accomplishes two goals: It sets them on the path to having disciplined savings deposits and it also allows them some freedom to decide if they want to spend or save a portion of their "income." When they are adults, they will be making these same choices on a daily basis and will be setting aside a fixed, recurring amount every month to fund their retirement plans or emergency fund.

When I was growing up, I never really had any allowance or other money coming in. I didn't have any expenses either because my grandparents bought me anything I wanted or needed. The concept of kids dealing with money was a foreign concept in my family. It wasn't until I got out on my own at 17 that I realized I needed a financial education—and quick! I made a ton of mistakes along the way that hurt me financially but I'm doing much better now. I only hope that I can prevent my kids from making the same mistakes.

~ CHARLOTTE P., CAMROSE, ALBERTA

✓ CHANGING SAVINGS GOALS

Like adults, kids will likely change their wants and needs many times and will want to re-adjust their savings goals. Walking them through the process of deciding whether new goals are more appropriate will help them to make these types of decisions in the future. If you instead hold them to their original plans ("you wanted the iPod so you have to keep saving for it"), kids can lose interest in savings. That doesn't mean that they should change their goals every few days when something new and cool comes on the market. Help them to put some real thought into why the new goals make more sense now than the current goals. Then, help them figure out how much more or less they will have to save on a regular basis to adjust to the new goal.

The Royal Canadian Mint produces approximately 760,000,000 one-cent coins annually.

✓ TRANSITIONING FROM PIGGY BANK TO BANK BOOK

Your kids can't go around saving money in a canning jar forever (although I still love my penny jar!). Once they have had a few years of experience handling money, budgeting, and saving, they're ready to understand how a bank account works. Most banks offer children's accounts with no monthly fees to eat away at their savings. If your bank doesn't have this option, shop around a bit (and, really, who wants to stay with a bank that charges kids fees for saving money?). Once you have found a no-fee account, look at the update options. Some accounts will send monthly statements and some will have bank books. If you have a choice, choose the bank book option so that kids can easily see a complete history of their growing fund.

Most banks will require that parents are signatories on the accounts of minor children. Don't make the account require two signatures for withdrawals, however. The money in the savings account should be as much under the control of your child as the piggy bank was. Needing mom or dad to sign off takes that control away. The exception to this is long-term savings. If a child has an account set up for college or other long-term goals, it is wise to require your signature as well as your child's for withdrawals. It protects your children from making impetuous and financially harming decisions.

> Inflation hasn't ruined everything. A dime can still be used as a screwdriver.
> ~Quoted in P.S. I Love You, compiled by H. Jackson Brown, Jr.

Once kids are ready to transfer their savings money over to a bank account, it's time to amalgamate the separate savings buckets. Kids can still keep track of their separate goals on paper but it makes sense to keep all of the funds in a single account. The exception to this is university or college savings. In both Canada and the United States, there are government-sponsored savings options that can give college funds a tax-advantaged boost, and it often makes more sense to save those funds in this type of account. There is more information on these types of accounts later in this chapter.

✓ WHY MOVE TO A BANK ACCOUNT?

When it's time to make the transition from piggy bank to bank account, your kids may ask why and it's a valid question. Why do we keep money in bank accounts rather than under our mattress or behind the stove? You may think the answers are obvious, but not necessarily to kids who have never been exposed to the banking system before. Here are the main benefits of keeping money in the bank:

◉ *Money is physically secure*

If you have money stuffed in your pillowcase at home, it is at risk of loss. Remember, it's nothing more than bits of paper. A stack of bills is at risk if there is a flood or fire or other catastrophe that could damage it. It's not a replaceable asset. You can't exchange soggy bits of a hundred-dollar bill for a new one. Banks provide physical security for your money. Money on hand is kept in a theft-proof and fire-proof vault. It is accessible from almost anywhere in the world.

② *The balance earns interest*

All savings accounts pay interest to depositors for the privilege of using the money to loan to other customers. When saving in a piggy bank, the money never grows on its own. With interest, the balance grows more quickly.

③ *It builds up your financial history*

At some point in almost everyone's life, they need to borrow money or establish credit-worthiness. A lender looks at your entire financial history to decide whether you are a good risk. A lengthy bank account ownership shows a lender that you can handle money appropriately. They can't tell that if you keep your money in a coffee jar.

④ *It provides proof of transactions*

If you pay for something in cash and lose the receipt, you have no way of proving that you paid. In order to return items to stores or to make a warranty claim, you

Security threads, made of metal foil or plastic, are imbedded into many paper currencies to prevent counterfeiting. These strips are difficult to replicate and provide extra security to the currency.

almost always need proof of purchase. A debit in the bank account shows the exact amount and date paid.

⑤ *Personal safety*

Carrying around wads of cash is inherently dangerous. You risk robbery or even personal injury. If you are known for keeping large sums of money in your house, your home may become a target for thieves. Keeping your cash in the bank is safer. Even if a thief gets hold of your ATM or debit card, your bank will put a freeze on the account. If money is stolen before you report the theft, the bank will likely replace it.

Kids may ask you about the reliability of the bank. Younger kids often phrase it in terms of "what happens if the banker steals my money" while older kids know that the real concern is what happens if the bank goes under. You can ease their minds by explaining bank insurance.

In Canada, the Canada Deposit Insurance Corporation (CDIC) insures bank balances up to $100,000 per depositor per institution. CDIC is a Crown corporation created by Parliament in 1967 (Canada's Centennial year) to protect deposits made with member financial institutions in case of their failure.

This means that if you have $50,000 in savings at a bank and it becomes insolvent, the CDIC will step in and pay you $50,000. The insurance premiums are paid by the member banks and your deposits are automatically covered. Not all investments are CDIC-insured, for example, equity investments, so check with your bank to ensure that your savings vehicles are covered. If you have more than $100,000 in savings, it makes sense to hold it at multiple banks to avoid losses above the CDIC cap.

My problem lies in reconciling my gross habits with my net income.
~Errol Flynn

In the United States, the Federal Deposit Insurance Corporation (FDIC) is a federal corporation born in the midst of the Great Depression. It insures bank deposits for member institutions up to $250,000 per depositor per institution. As in Canada, not all investments are FDIC-insured, so take time to make certain that your investments are eligible for FDIC insurance. Because of the decentralization of the U.S. banking system and the lower levels of required capitalization for banks, it is even more important in the U.S. than in Canada to make sure that your money is covered under FDIC insurance. Bank failures occur often, especially with small regional banks, making the role of the FDIC critical.

✓ CANADA-REGISTERED EDUCATION SAVINGS PLAN

Canada's registered education savings plan (RESP) provides lots of benefits to those saving for university. The overall maximum allowable contributions are $50,000 per beneficiary but contributions in any amount can be made up to that maximum. One of the best parts of an RESP is that the government will kick some in, too. A Canada Education Savings Grant (CESG) matches 20 percent of your annual contributions up to a maximum annual grant of $500. Middle- and lower-income families receive even higher grants. The total amount of grant in the lifetime of each plan is $7,200. The contributions are not tax-deductible but the withdrawals are made in the child's name. They will pay tax on the income portion of the withdrawal, but the vast majority of university students have low income and high tuition credits, in which case they won't pay tax on the withdrawals. When it comes time to withdraw money from an RESP, the subscriber (usually the parent) is the only one who is able to request funds from the plan. You can direct the payment of the total of the contributions to either you or your child, but the grant and income portion must be paid to the child. You still control when and how much the withdrawals are.

> Every day I get up and look through the Forbes list of the richest people in America. If I'm not there, I go to work.
> ~Robert Orben

✓ U.S.-529 PLANS

These plans are allowed by the Internal Revenue Service (IRS) but are administered on a state-by-state basis. Each state's plan works a little differently. The basic premise is that you can fund the plan until the child goes to college and then withdraw the principal and income tax-free. Although you (or your child) will not get a federal tax deduction on the contributions, you will never pay tax on the income, as long as it is used for education purposes. Some states also offer separate state tax breaks for contributions. Limits on contributions are very high (over $300,000 in some states) and you—as the parent—retain full control of the account.

When my son was born and on his first few birthdays, he received a number of small-denomination savings bonds. When he was about eight, he had accumulated about $800 in value. I added $200 to make the minimum amount to open a custodial stock-trading account in his name. We discussed each stock purchase and sale and agreed that the principal and stock value growth would be saved for college expenses, but that he could take 50% of any dividends out to spend; the rest was reinvested. We have never added to the account, but in his best year, he pulled out $1400 in dividends to spend. The regular checks from dividends showed him the value of long-term holding of solid investments. Although the dividends have dropped dramatically in this economy, he is adamant about doing everything he can to keep his stocks and not liquidate the fund for college.

My child is heading to college this fall and, at 18 years old, he is eager to get a credit card. I support that in order to begin establishing credit. We have discussed the folly of spending money you don't have and he assures me he will not use credit for things that he cannot pay for before the bill is due. I suspect he will carry a balance at some point during his college years, but I'm confident that he won't let it get out of control. Still, I worry.

~ BRAD S., STRAFFORD, NEW HAMPSHIRE

✓ CALCULATING THE COST OF UNIVERSITY
OR COLLEGE

Trying to figure out how much it will actually cost to send your child to college or university can make you tear your hair out. As both an accountant and the mother of a son in his junior year of high school, it is an issue discussed frequently in our household. While many colleges focus on disclosing the full cost of tuition, there are many other costs that need to be considered when budgeting for college.

College Sticker Price

This is the full price of tuition for a college and the number most often revealed on a college's Web site. This figure does not include any scholarships or student aid based on needs or merit. The sticker price is rarely the price actually paid, as most colleges offer automatic grants and scholarships to incoming students with high grades. According to a recent *Washington Post* article, seeing only the full sticker price of a college can keep many students from applying to their desired colleges, even though the net price would be very affordable.

> When I was young I thought that money was the most important thing in life; now that I am old I know that it is.
> ~Oscar Wilde

Student Aid

Student aid comes in many forms. Colleges offer merit- and needs-based scholarships to many or even all of their first year students. Private and corporate scholarships are also available to most students based on academic record. In Canada, federal and provincial grants and loans are offered based on financial need. In the United States, the federal government offers the HOPE scholarship based on high school test scores. Loans and grants make up the rest of student aid. When considering the price of college tuition, it is important to deduct the benefits of student aid so that you understand the true out-of-pocket cost.

Books and Resource Material

I remember the first time I walked into the university bookstore and bought a copy of my first-year accounting textbook. I don't remember how much I thought it should have cost, but I just about passed out cold when I saw that it was $132. I ate mostly Ramen noodles and rice for the rest of that month to make up for the cost of books. This is a cost that is often forgotten about or grossly underestimated. In some college programs, a single textbook could cost several hundred dollars. As more colleges begin to feel financial pressures, resource material such as study packages and handouts are being sold rather than included in the tuition cost of courses. Books and resource material can cost upwards of one-quarter to one-half of the tuition cost itself. Sometimes, buying used textbooks can ease this financial burden but many courses require the current year's edition of a textbook—especially if the professor is the one who wrote it!

Room and Board

Living expenses make up the bulk of the rest of college costs. Many college students choose to live in residence for the first year and then live off-campus with friends in subsequent ones. Residence costs are often higher than private living arrangements, especially if meal plans are included and there are no cooking facilities. Regardless of where your child will live during college, you will need to calculate all room-and-board costs, such as rent, utilities, parking, and laundry.

Transportation

If your child will be going to college in an urban area with a robust public transportation system, he may never need a car. The transportation cost to factor in is simply the cost of the transportation pass. If a car is needed, all of the related costs must be figured in, such as payments, gas, repairs and maintenance, and parking.

> If you think nobody cares if you're alive, try missing a couple of car payments.
> ~Earl Wilson

✓ THE BASICS OF INTEREST

We'll talk more about the banking system in Chapter Seven, "Piggy Banks & Plastic: Teaching Kids About Banking and Credit," but it's a good idea to give kids an overview of how interest works when they set up their first savings account.

To find the number of years it would take to double your investment at any particular interest rate, use the rule of 72. Divide the interest rate into 72 to arrive at the number of years it will take to double your money. For example, if you invest your money at 6 percent annual interest, it will take 12 years for it to double (72/6=12).

The easiest way to explain interest to kids for the first time is often by using an example. Joan wants to deposit $100 in a bank account. The bank takes Joan's $100 and loans it to Frank, who needs to borrow money for his small business. The bank offers Joan $3 a year to keep her deposit in the bank. It charges Frank $6 a year to borrow money. Joan is happy because she makes $3 on her money. Frank is happy because he gets to borrow money he wouldn't otherwise have available to him. The bank is happy because it gets to pocket the difference of $3. That is one way the bank earns a return for its shareholders—by lending out deposits.

A question my daughter asked when she was first learning about how interest works was what happens if Joan wants her money out of the account before Frank can pay it back. The bank looks at its deposits and lending as a whole. It's not really

Joan's money that funds Frank; it's the total deposits in the bank. Banks are required to keep a certain ratio of deposits on hand to the total amount of their lending. This keeps banks solvent and goes a long way toward avoiding the bank failures seen in the wake of the Great Depression.

Kids who have a strong math background can also understand the concept of compound interest. Again, this is best explained with an example. Let's say Joan, above, gets her $3 in interest at the end of the year. She now has a total of $103 in her bank account. If she leaves that sum in the account for another year, she will earn interest not only on the original $100 but also on the interest from year 1. Instead of making $3 (at 3 percent annual interest), she'll make $3.09. It doesn't seem like much on a hundred dollars but it adds up quickly as your savings grow.

✓ ALTERNATIVE SAVINGS VEHICLES

Once the transition from piggy bank to bank account is complete, it's time to talk to your kids about other forms of savings. The savings account will pay a tiny pittance in interest but long-term savings goals can be saved for in other types of investments that give a higher return.

> Car sickness is the feeling you get when the monthly payment is due.
> ~Author Unknown

I'm not talking about getting your kids into the stock market (at least, not right away). I'm talking about fixed-term investments such as Guaranteed Investment Certificates (GICs) in Canada, Certificates of Deposit (CDs) in the U.S. or government savings bonds.

Banks pay higher rates of interest on locked-in deposits. If the bank knows that it can keep your deposit for a year or five years without you wanting it back, it can do more with those funds and, therefore, is willing to pay more in interest.

Guaranteed Investment Certificates and Certificates of Deposit are offered by banks for fixed terms, usually from 6 months to 5 years. They are secured by deposit insurance in both countries and represent one of the safest fixed-rate investments. They can be cashed-in early in an emergency but there is usually a penalty for doing so which makes it an unattractive option. Most GICs and CDs carry a fixed rate of interest but some are based on stock market performance, which makes their overall return less certain. In general, the larger the amount of money deposited and the longer the term, the higher the interest rate. This may not hold true if recession is on the horizon. In recessionary times, the expectation of high interest rates in the future is diminished, so shorter term interest rates may actually be higher than longer term rates.

> Always borrow money from a pessimist, he doesn't expect to be paid back.
> ~Author Unknown

Once your kids have defined their savings buckets, they can improve their overall return on their longer-term savings by investing in GICs or CDs. For example, if your child has $1,000 saved for university in five years, she can purchase a GIC or CD for a five-year term. The deposit and its accumulated interest will be available in time to use the funds for school. Alternatively, she can invest it for one-year terms and reinvest every year.

Government bonds are another option. Bonds can be issued by any level of government, from federal down to municipalities to raise funds for projects. Federal bonds are secured by the ability of the government to raise taxes if necessary to pay back the funds and are considered to be practically risk-free. Bonds issued by smaller units of government are only as safe as the government unit itself. With recent revenue crises in several states and cities across North America, these bonds have become a riskier proposition. Sticking with federally-issued bonds is the safest option for your kids' savings.

✓ SUMMARY

- Young children need to keep the money they handle as tangible and real as possible. Watching money physically grow in a jar or a piggy bank will help kids understand the process of saving and spending more so than reading lines in a bank book.

> Money may be the husk of many things but not the kernel. It brings you food, but not appetite; medicine, but not health; acquaintance, but not friends; servants, but not loyalty; days of joy, but not peace or happiness.
> ~Henrik Ibsen

- Not all savings are the same. Kids, like adults, need separate "buckets" for short-term saving, long-term or college saving, and current spending. For younger children, these "buckets" can actually be separate piggy banks or jars. For older kids, this partitioning can occur on paper.

- Helping your children set savings goals assists them in making cost/benefit or value judgments. They will make spending decisions they regret, but they will learn from each mistake.

- Canadian RESPs and American 529 plans have benefits to help kids and their parents save for university or college. Some plans offer the benefit of being tax-deferred, which allows the savings to grow more quickly than if it was taxed. Some plans also have government contributions attached. They are an important part of the post-secondary portion of savings.

- When kids begin to grow their long-term savings, they can begin to explore investment options that pay higher interest rates, including Guaranteed Investment Certificates and Certificates of Deposit.

RACHEL'S STORY

My 17-year-old has had a savings account at a credit union since he was too young to do banking. Gifts in the form of checks always went in there and never came out. He's had experience investing this money in short-term Certificates of Deposit and seeing what higher interest rates do. He learned about dropping interest rates and when it's good or not good to invest money, too. When the credit union allowed checking and debit cards at 15, he got them. He writes checks for certain things at school and uses his debit card online and in stores. He doesn't have a line of credit for overspending. If the debit card is declined, he can just stand there and be embarrassed! He was taught how to check his statements and do all his own banking. If something happens to me, he will be able to take over the household finances without a problem. I've monitored his accounts up until now and he's never gone on a spending spree or abused his right to hold a debit card in any way. Financial intelligence and building credit has to start at an early age! Starting a kid with a credit card when they go away to college and are away from home for the first time is asking for trouble.

My son has never had any spending limits, but knew when the money was gone, it was gone. He didn't like to see the balance drop, so he was careful not to spend it unwisely. He would save for game consoles that he wanted but we wouldn't buy for him, so he learned something about saving, even though he didn't have regular bills to budget for.

My son is prepared, but I would like to discuss more with him the fact that not all banks and credit unions are the same. Some have stricter rules about issuing credit than others. Some have more fees than others, and it's important to know if you'll have a fee charged if your account drops below a certain balance. On one account, he has a reminder set up for when he gets close to that amount so he can act accordingly and not be charged a fee. Nothing is left to chance.

My son has access to my banking and will be on the accounts when he turns 18, instead of waiting for the pile of red tape if something should happen to me. He knows how to enter bills for auto-payment so they're never late, and how to make transfers. I'm confident that if I wasn't able to do the financial work here, he could step in and no one would be the wiser. We do almost everything online, including check deposits with a phone app.

My son no longer has any limits or need for approval, but he will often discuss purchases before he makes them. I've found myself discussing purchases with him, and he's been able to make money-saving recommendations, so I'm very confident that he is a savvy consumer and won't be duped by Internet schemes and high pressure salespeople!

Moving back in with me as an adult depends on the economy and circumstances. There's no such thing as a free lunch here if he were to move back. He would pay what was within his means, even if it was a small amount. It's the principle. He could live with me until he was stable enough to live independently. I wouldn't push him out before he was ready and cause a relapse. That said, he's preparing himself for a financially stable career and has shown he is responsible handling his finances up to now, so I'm hoping he'll never be in a situation where he'll have to move home. I might have to move in with HIM!

My son isn't responsible for any of his university expenses. My husband was forced to work and pay for his education and the struggle and hunger of those years won't fade from his memory. He wants our son to focus on his classes, get enough rest, and enjoy the experience rather than be stressed and tired. However, he is expected to keep his grades up so he can get into the organizations that are good for networking and career building. Without the burden of a job to pay his own expenses, he's excelling at school and will graduate with a BA in Psychology next May, then go on to grad school. By financing his education, we feel he will have a career that will always bring in a good income so he won't have to worry about how he'll pay his bills...as long as he lives within his means.

~ RACHEL D., SANTA BARBARA, CALIFORNIA

CHAPTER SIX

Paying the Piper: Teaching Kids About Wise Spending

✓ INTRODUCTION

Teaching kids to spend can be infinitely more difficult than teaching them how to save. It can sometimes be tempting not to talk about spending money at all, in hopes that they won't do it. But, as we all know, kids want to spend some of their hard-earned money just like we want to spend some of ours. The best thing that you can do for your kids is to teach them to spend it wisely.

One concept that many kids don't intuitively understand when they see the spending money in their piggy banks or in their bank accounts growing is that they don't have to spend. Not all of it and not right now. It's not going to disappear if they hang onto it and wait until they are certain what they want to spend it on. Some kids are in such a hurry to exchange their money for something else, they end up regretting what they bought in haste.

That's where you step in as a parent. Children need to learn how to maneuver their way through the quicksand of the advertising they're bombarded with every day and decide amongst many choices what they want to spend their own money on. To do this, they will need to develop their critical evaluation skills to look at the benefits and potential downsides of each potential purchase. They will make mistakes along the way but they will learn from them and make better choices as adults, when the stakes are much higher.

> There are people who have money and people who are rich.
> ~Coco Chanel

✓ THE SCOURGE OF ADVERTISING

"Mom, you should get X brand of dishwashing detergent. It works five times better than other brands."

Do you ever have those types of conversations at your house? When my kids were small, they knew every ad on all the kids' television channels. They could recite them verbatim and sing the jingles. It didn't seem to matter whether the commercial was touting toys or...dishwasher detergent. They had them all memorized. When they began watching television shows on non-children-oriented channels, I started to get questions about what depression and erectile dysfunction were. Why is it that kids pay attention to ads, often above paying attention to their parents?

① *Small children often don't understand what a commercial is.*

While it's clear to adults that commercials are paid for by companies to flog a product, young kids frequently mistake them for part of the show they're watching. They don't understand the difference between programming and paid programming. This gives ads credibility with kids that ads often don't deserve. Kids think that, if it's on television, it must be true.

❷ *Ads are relentless.*

According to the American Academy of Pediatrics, kids are exposed to over 40,000 advertisements per year on television alone. And that's just ad spots. Now, companies are paying to have product placement in the shows themselves, so kids see their favorite characters and actors favoring one brand over another, which subtly affects their brand perceptions.

> Too much money is as demoralizing as too little, and there's no such thing as exactly enough.
> ~Mignon McLaughlin, The Second Neurotic's Notebook, 1966

Ads are also becoming more common on the Internet, on electronic reading devices, in schools, and even in church. Kids are literally bombarded with sales pitches from the time they wake up in the morning until the time they go to bed. No wonder they become walking, talking billboards as soon as they're able to talk.

❸ *Ads sell lifestyle.*

Advertisers have become very adept at not only selling a product or service, but selling the promise of a better life. This happens in ads aimed at both kids and adults. Buy X brand of disinfectant spray and your family will be relaxed and happy. Buy Y brand of jeans and you'll have more friends at school and be more popular. Adults have a difficult enough time fighting off these embedded perceptions. Kids don't stand a chance. If they're led to believe that having an mp3 player makes them cool, it's hard for parents to break that perception.

So, what's the answer? Never allowing your kids to watch television, listen to the radio, pick up a magazine, or go online? Of course not— in fact, that only makes them less ad-savvy. The more you teach your kids to be wise, if not outright cynical, consumers of advertising, the better they will be able to filter out the noise in the future.

Your kids will have to be able to analyze commercial advertising when they get older and determine the appropriateness and truthfulness of it on their own.

Here are 7 things that you can help your kids to understand about commercials:

① The payments made by advertisers to the television network, radio station, or magazine (the media) are what make the other programming possible.

② The media do not endorse or agree with advertisers. As long as they are following basic laws, ads can say what they want. Just because an ad for a restaurant appears during a Waltons re-run, it doesn't mean that John Boy likes the restaurant. It may seem self-evident to us, but to young children, it is a difficult concept.

The penny loafer got its name in the 1950s from the common practice in American prep schools of inserting a penny into the diamond-shaped cutout in the front of slip-on shoes. The fashion statement caught on and is still in evidence today.

(3) Advertisers make many claims that have no objective proof or data to back them up. There are some governing bodies that regulate television advertising and some industry controls, such as in the drug industry, about what companies can claim, but, by and large, it's still the Wild West when it comes to the miracles that companies can claim come from using their products or services.

(4) Words like "best," "more," "larger," "cheaper," "sale," "half off," and "free shipping" do not necessarily mean what they suggest. Those are the weasel words of advertising that lead consumers to believe that the product or service is better than other choices.

(5) While there are some great direct-to-consumer products sold over the telephone through television advertising, the industry has a reputation for hidden fees and exorbitant processing and handling fees. More research about products should always be done before purchasing from a commercial.

(6) The word "guarantee" is only as strong as the company offering it. If the company is fly-by-night and gone next month, a lifetime guarantee is meaningless.

(7) Food advertising doesn't represent what kids should be eating on a regular basis. Most food advertising is for high-calorie, high-sugar, or high-fat foods that give advertisers a high profit margin. Everything from sugary cereals to breakfast pastries to soda are marketed relentlessly to kids.

It is unlikely your children will see ads for salads and roast chicken. Kids should understand that highly processed convenience foods shouldn't be an everyday occurrence, even though they see advertising for it every day.

Start by sitting with your children and watching some ads together. Ask them what impressions they have about each product and what it was the ad said to give them that impression. What did the ad tell them about the reliability or usefulness of the product? How do your kids see themselves using it and for how long?

Point out the weasel words to them and show them where the dangers lie in ads. My daughter and I have a game where, every time an ad on television says "shipping and handling" or "processing," we both yell "ha" and see who does it first.

> People are living longer than ever before, a phenomenon undoubtedly made necessary by the 30-year mortgage.
> ~Doug Larson

Own up to your own purchasing mistakes. When I was younger, I loved to buy kitchen gadgets. I had a bunch of them and still use some of them to this day. I still have two juicers, a sandwich press, and a deep-fryer hiding in the back of my kitchen cupboards, unused and unloved. Making fresh juice every day was going to make my life amazing. I found it was only a giant time-waster and the machines were hard to clean. Pull your own mistakes out of closets and cupboards and basements. Explain to your children your reasoning for buying them in the first place and what your expectations were. Then tell them why the products didn't live up to those expectations (broke down, hard to use, or obsolete, for example). Again, kids will learn from your bad decisions as much or more as from your good ones.

The final lesson that will set kids on the right path when they want to buy something they see advertised is research. Kids as young as eight can go on the Internet and research products. They can find out what people who have already bought them think about them. They can compare features against similar products. They can also find out where to get the best price. Thoughtful and researched spending can save your children tens of thousands of dollars over their lifetime. Help them set up this important money habit early.

When I was a young girl, the Sears & Roebuck Company published their Wish Book catalogue every fall for the Christmas season. It came in a plain brown paper sleeve and smelled gloriously of printers' ink and anticipation. It was full of toys and gift items and was just like a virtual trip to the toy aisle that city kids got to have all the time. Those of us who lived out in the country waited on the book every year. I dog-eared the pages before Halloween came and had the book full of marked pages and circled dreams before the end of November. I always managed to convince Santa Claus to bring me a few of the book's wondrous offerings, but there were always toys I still really wanted after Christmas. The Wish Book was my guide to my spending budget. I prioritized what I wanted in list after list and projected out how long it would take me to save up for it. There were always a few things left over to ask Santa for the next year.

~ CHLOE P., CORNER BROOK, NEWFOUNDLAND

✓ LESSONS OF THE GROCERY STORE

One of the first ways most kids get hands-on experience with money and budgeting is at the grocery store. It is a great opportunity to help them hone their smart spending skills. It may be tempting to leave kids at home and save yourself the headache of juggling grocery shopping and a few cases of the "gimmes," but kids learn all kinds of real-life financial and non-financial lessons when you let them help you in the grocery store.

> Budget: a mathematical confirmation of your suspicions.
> ~A.A. Latimer

✓ FIVE GROCERY STORE LESSONS FOR KIDS:

Comparative math

Letting your children decide whether the big "economy" box of cereal is a better deal than the smaller one helps them sharpen their math skills with real-life scenarios and also helps them to learn how to bargain hunt. It may seem self-evident that bigger packages are always less expensive per unit than smaller ones but this frequently isn't the case. My husband sometimes even has a difficult time with this concept. Show your kids how to compare unit prices. Most grocery stores show the price per unit (gram, pound, roll, etc.) on the shelf tags to make comparisons easy. The shelf tags are not always correct, but they're a good start for younger children to look at. Older kids can do the division themselves. They don't have to do it all in their head. Let them bring calculators with them to the store to calculate unit price. Unit price is simply the total cost divided by the units presented. For example, if a package of ground coffee is $4.19 for 12 ounces, its cost can be expressed as $4.19/12=35$ cents (rounded) per ounce. The large size bag of coffee might be 2 pounds (which converts to 32 ounces). If that bag goes for $12.15, that works out to $12.15/32=38 cents per ounce. When comparing 35 cents to 38 cents, the smaller size package is less expensive per unit.

Choose four or five items on your grocery list ahead of time that you will get your kids to "do the math" on when you get to the store. Most kids love to be able to figure out the answer to the riddle. Just make sure you also know the answer so that you know if they're right!

Selection

Allow kids to go through the sale flyers with you before your shopping trip. Talk to them about what's on sale and approximately what the regular price would be so that they can judge whether it's a good sale or not. Remind them that, just because something is "on sale," it's just another weasel word and that they can't determine if it's a good deal or not without knowing what it costs normally. This is a good opportunity to talk to them about needs versus wants. Just because candy bars are 50 percent off this week at your local grocery store, it doesn't mean that you should buy them. A sale is only a bargain if it's something you would buy anyway.

If you lend someone $20, and never see that person again, it was probably worth it.
~Author unknown

You can introduce your children to food storage in this process. Knowing how to buy and store food will save your kids thousands of dollars over the years when they are adults. You don't have to talk about it in elaborate detail, especially with younger children, but, for example, you could explain why you're buying eight steaks this week (because they're 50 percent off) and freezing some rather than buying a variety of meats for the week's meals. Explain that, next week, chicken might be on sale and then you'll stock up on that.

While reviewing the grocery sale flyers with your kids and coming up with a grocery list, discuss the concept of loss leaders with them. Loss leaders are those grocery items that are offered at a deep discount to lure customers into the store and, hopefully, get them to buy lots of other things. Loss leaders are often featured on the front page of flyers and are marked down significantly. Shopping the loss leaders without buying all kinds of full price groceries at the same time can really stretch the budget (which we'll talk about in the next section).

Paper money in the U.S. and Canada isn't made out of paper. It is made from a weave of cotton and linen and stands up longer than paper would.

Estimation

This is another skill that kids can learn while helping you to build your grocery list from the sale flyer. If there is a great sale on something you use regularly, you have to determine how many of them you want. For example, my husband only uses one brand of hair conditioner and, when it goes on sale, I have to decide how many to pick up. Part of the decision is based on the sale discount (if it's 30 cents off, I know that it regularly goes on sale for a dollar off, so I won't pick up many). Part of it is based on sales cycles. Savvy grocery shoppers know that certain items go on sale on a cycle; for example, every month or every four months. If the deal is a good one, you will want to pick up enough to last you until it goes on sale again. The last part of the decision is based on perishability. If apples go on sale for half price, there's no point picking up a bushel unless you're going to somehow preserve them. Overbuying sale items and wasting them doesn't save any money in the long run.

Have your kids help you decide how many of certain sale items to buy. See if they know how long it takes the family to go through a bottle of shampoo or a loaf of bread. Discuss the sales cycles and how long things last. When kids (and adults!) start really trying to shop the bargains at the grocery store, they tend to buy too many of some things and then feel guilty because some gets wasted. Help your kids learn how to balance saving money on groceries with realistic spending.

Couponing

Couponing is all the rage these days. It was always something my grandmother did— diligently clipping coupons for 25 cents off here and 15 cents off there. Growing up, I always secretly thought it was an old-fashioned pursuit that took more time than it was worth. But, as always, Grandma was right— and families all over Canada and the U.S. are getting their scissors out.

Matching up flyer sales with coupons can save an average of around 40% on your overall grocery bill. Spend some time with your kids clipping coupons for groceries you buy on a regular basis. You can even let your children take the lead by having them set up a three-ring binder with clear plastic sheets to sort and store coupons. If your child asks you why you bother, ask him if he would throw away a couple of quarters he found on the sidewalk or a crumpled dollar bill lying in the playground. The answer will likely be "no." Explain how coupons are just as valuable as money for those items you already buy. Why pay $2 for something when you can get it for $1.50? Couponing is a great skill for kids to learn because they have to practice all of their other grocery store skills to do it the right way.

Restraint

Walk into any grocery store and watch parents with young children. You'll witness all different kinds of behavior. There will be the parents who let their children run free in the store to keep them occupied and not underfoot. You'll see parents involving their children in the shopping process, helping them pick out groceries and read the list. Then you will likely see the "gimme kids"—those kids who have learned that if they ask long enough and make a big enough and loud enough commotion in the store, their parents will give them anything they want. This book is not specifically a parenting book, but it will help you not to have "gimme kids." An important grocery store lesson for kids is to learn restraint—that they can't have every toy, chocolate bar, and bag of chips they want.

> By the time I have money to burn, my fire will have burnt out.
> ~Author Unknown

As with any other type of spending, spending at the grocery store requires planning. You have a budget set ahead of time. Your kids should, too. Allowing them to spend a small amount of money when they shop with you forces them to make decisions about what it is they really want. Would they rather have that magazine or ice cream cone? Give them a dollar or two limit and stick to your guns. Physically hand them the money so that they are clear on the fact that it is all they are getting. Better yet, allow them to spend that dollar or two from their own earned spending money. Kids will make more calculated and thoughtful choices if they have to part with their own funds. Make sure they can calculate the taxes on anything they buy so they know what their real spending limit is, providing them with another opportunity to practice math skills.

I prefer to discuss purchases on a case-by-case basis, rather than making rules. It's difficult to set a one-size-fits-all protocol for purchases. When our children make a purchase, we do a Plus-Minus Inventory, also called cost-benefit analysis. I'm not so concerned about cost as I am value. We do PMIs with luxury and necessity purchases.

~ MARILISA S., GRAND HAVEN, MICHIGAN

✓ INTRODUCING THE CONCEPT OF BUDGETING

As kids learn more about earning, saving, and spending money, they will bring all three of these skills together when they start learning about budgets. We'll look at the budgeting process more in-depth in Chapter Twelve, where you will help your kids put together their own spending budgets.

The first and most basic budgeting lesson that children need to learn is that no spending occurs before budgeting. That goes back to the concept of "every dollar has a name." Even small purchases should be pre-planned. That doesn't mean that every time your son wants to buy a comic book, he has to budget for the purchase. But it should come out of money that has been earmarked for current spending.

The first experience your kids should get with budgets is understanding your family budget. When you talk about what is and is not in the budget with your children, they begin to understand that money is a scarce commodity that needs to be actively managed. You don't have to sit down and present a Power Point show on the inner workings of the family budget. Telling kids things like how much is in the budget to spend at the grocery store that week, or how much the power bill cost over what was budgeted because of the heat wave, helps them to start relating abstract money concepts to real-life situations.

Once kids start earning their own money, whether through allowance or through their own entrepreneurial endeavors, they will have to apportion it between current spending, and short-term and long-term savings. In Chapter Five, we looked at how kids can manage the savings portion. Budgeting will help them manage their spending.

A man is usually more careful of his money than of his principles.
~Oliver Wendell Holmes, Jr., speech, Boston, 8 January 1897

✓ WHO'S IN CHARGE?

When each of my kids started earning allowance and getting birthday and holiday money from grandparents and other relatives, they naturally wanted to start spending it. We talked about saving money and set up savings plans for the kids but they still had money they were allowed to spend. Invariably, at least when they were still young, they wanted to spend their money on things that my husband and I thought were ridiculous. Ten packs of Pokemon cards. Or five bottles of glitter nail polish. A bag of Slim Jims and Japanese comic books. Or something equally as fleeting and depreciable. As an accountant and a mother, my first urge was to kibosh the whole thing and make sure my kids chose their spending targets better. I'm glad I learned to rein in my own controlling nature over time and allowed my kids to be in charge of their own spending. That doesn't mean that I let them buy absolutely anything they want without thinking about it. I help to guide their decisions by listening to their thought processes about why they chose those things and helping them to come to the best decisions for them.

Have my kids made mistakes? Oh, yes. However, the money spent was minimal and they learned from every mistake. There's nothing like wishing you had the money back rather than the hot new toy from six months ago that's now boring and passé to teach you to spend more wisely the next time. Allowing kids to make wrong financial decisions is far more helpful and containable now than when they buy their first home. Let them pilot the ship on their spending once you have agreed with their overall spending and savings plan. You can still be their co-pilot.

My daughter's summer job paid bi-weekly. I made her put half the pay in the bank. She could use the rest of her money any way she wanted. But she was responsible for buying her own lunches. The group she worked with went to lunch at least twice a week. I felt this taught her better budgeting skills.

~ JULIE R., CARROLTON, OHIO

✓ THE 24-HOUR RULE

One way to help your kids make better spending decisions is by instituting the 24-Hour Rule. The rule goes something like this: they may decide what to spend their money on as long as they wait at least 24 hours between the time they decide and when they make the purchase. This prevents the inevitable impulse purchasing that would otherwise happen. It's easy to pull money out of their wallets when they first see something they think they want. Novelty is a powerful spending motivator. The 24-hour interval gives them time for sober second thought and allows them to consider alternative purchases that they might ultimately want instead. It also gives them time to look the item up online and find out more information about it, including customer reviews and average prices.

If you make the 24-Hour Rule a part of your child's spending plan, it will give them more opportunities to make good choices and will give you more peace of mind knowing that they have put thought into the purchase.

✓ TITHING & DONATING

A portion of the spending done by many families is tithing and donating to charity. How you feel about these practices will have a large influence on what you teach your children about them.

Tithing, in its most basic form, is defined as giving a percentage of your income to a place of worship or to religious charities. It has been a Christian, Jewish, and Muslim tradition in different forms for thousands of years. Not all religious groups still practice tithing and, even for those who do, it is often a more voluntary and less mandated practice than it has been throughout history. Most Christian tithing practices call for 10 percent of your gross income from all sources to be donated to the church or to missionary endeavors. From a financial standpoint, tithing simply represents another line item in your budget, a non-discretionary expense that continues as long as you have income.

If tithing (or a similar practice) is a part of your family's faith and you want your children to be raised in the faith, teach them to tithe as soon as they start earning their own allowance or other money. Instead of splitting their earnings into spending, long-term and short-term savings, and donating, tithing will be a fifth category. If it is to be a percentage of the earnings, remove it first and then split up the rest into the other three categories. When your family attends services, your kids can take the tithe money from their jars or piggy banks and take it with them to put into the collection envelope.

Paper currency was first introduced by the U.S. federal government in 1861. The first bank notes had to be signed by hand by the Treasurer or his designees. It took six people working full time to sign all of the notes in circulation. Today, the signatures are imprinted onto the note.

Donating to charity on a regular basis is also a practice that many families feel strongly about, including ours. Charitable giving can take on many forms. It can be stuffing some change into the Salvation Army kettle at Christmas. It can be buying school supplies or canned goods for local charitable initiatives. It can even include "adopting" a foster child in another country and corresponding with her. Charitable giving doesn't have to be only financial, either. You can donate your time and talents to local charities to help them in their work. You can donate household goods and clothing to charitable thrift shops. Donating doesn't even have to involve a registered charity. Offering to cut your elderly neighbor's lawn or shovel his snow is a charitable act.

Your kids will take in how your family views charitable giving. If it is an important part of your family values, I recommend that you start your kids on the path of philanthropy early. Help them decide how they are going to help their community. It may be through a combination of volunteering their time and giving money.

Talk to your children about the charities that you support and why you choose to support them over the hundreds of other worthy organizations. However, don't force your choices on to them. If you support environmental charities and your children are showing interest in helping out the local pet shelter, allow them to explore their own interests and desires. They can always change how they spend their donation money in the future— it's not set in stone.

> The best way for a person to have happy thoughts is to count his blessings and not his cash.
> ~Author Unknown

One of the easiest ways to get them to donate regularly is to have them set it up as a separate jar or piggy bank and split any income they have coming in four ways. For example, 50 percent could be marked for current spending, 20 percent for short-term savings, 20 percent for long-term savings, and 10 percent for donations. When the donations jar builds up a certain balance, they can send that money to the charity. Alternatively, if it must be mailed, they can turn it over to you and you can mail the charity a check.

Whether it's tithing or charitable giving, teaching your kids to give back is an important lesson that they will take with them into adulthood.

I always had a job when I was growing up, since I was about eight. As I got older, the jobs paid more and were more demanding. By the time I was in high school, I would go up north tree-planting for the whole summer. It was the hardest work I have ever done in my life, but it paid extremely well and taught me how to live in a community. The money I made those summers paid for university. I worked part time as a teaching assistant during university, but didn't have to juggle a full work and school schedule because I planned ahead and saved most of my money. I want to be able to teach my kids how to do the same thing.

~ STEVEN R., PRINCE RUPERT, BRITISH COLUMBIA

✓ SUMMARY

- Children are bombarded with advertising on an increasing basis: on television, radio, the Internet, and in schools. Young children often cannot distinguish between television programming and advertising and it's important to help them to differentiate.

- The grocery store provides a great opportunity to give kids real-life financial lessons. They can learn comparative math, estimation, and budgeting, all in a single trip to the grocery store.

- Learning how to budget one's money appropriately can be a rocky experience for kids in the beginning. Not only do they have to decide between spending and savings, they have to decide what to spend on and what to save for. There will be mistakes made along the way, but they will lead to better decisions the next time.

- Even though it's important to let your children learn to budget for themselves, many families insist on a 24-Hour Rule. If a purchase is over a certain dollar amount, the child has to wait for a day to make sure she has had time to think it all the way through.

- Every family looks at tithing and donating differently. Charitable giving, whether to a religious institution or to charities, is important in many families. If it is a core value of yours, start your kids on the giving path as soon as they start saving their own money.

KATHY'S STORY

My son doesn't get a weekly allowance. I've spent a lot of time trying to make up for things in a monetary manner, so even when he did get an allowance, I still bought him the things he wanted. I changed the whole system so that now I can still buy him things "just because," but I put them up until such a time as he does something without being asked or does his chores without complaint. This means I still get to buy him things, but he has more appreciation for them and is more willing to do his chores.

He doesn't have a bank account, but he does have a savings plan here at home. When he earns money, 10 percent of it has to go into his savings box. He is free to do what he likes with the other 90 percent.

When my son is ready to leave home, I will help him to set up a budget based on a minimal income. I will also encourage him to put anything he earns above that minimal income in some sort of savings plan.

My son is only 10, so he has a limited concept of my earnings and bills. However, I have often thought about hanging up a chart that shows the incoming vs. the outgoing so he can develop a more realistic concept of what is taking place.

Doing side jobs is what earns my son extra money. He mows lawns and helps people in the community by doing odd jobs for them. Our school system provides teens 15 and older with job opportunities over the summer in the form of detassling corn. He will be participating in that when he's older.

My son has to compare prices and stop to think about whether or not the product is worth it in terms of quality as well as in terms of how much he will actually use it. In fact, I even have a rule that he has to haggle at yard sales before buying anything. Also, if he is going somewhere without me, he has to leave most of his money at home, mostly because he is very giving and will allow other people to spend it for him.

I would let my son or any stepchildren I may have in the future come home, with certain restrictions. I would make them pay rent, but I would put that in a savings plan (without their knowledge) that would later serve to help them get back on their feet. As far as indefinitely, it would depend on the situation. I would not financially support any adult indefinitely, but if the situation was based on being mutually beneficial or if the child could physically or mentally no longer care for themselves then, yes, I would do so indefinitely.

My parents had no part in paying for my college education and it helped me to develop character and appreciation. I don't plan to pay for my son's for that reason and more. I want him to have calluses on his hands before he's ever in a position to manage people that have calluses on their hands. The only way to ever truly appreciate the work that someone does is to have done it yourself.

~ KATHY F., HAMLET, INDIANA

CHAPTER SEVEN

Piggy Banks & Plastic: Teaching Kids About Banking & Credit

✓ INTRODUCTION

Younger children learn about working with money by physically handling it. Earning, spending, and saving all make more sense when real money changes hands and they can see those dimes, quarters, and dollar bills add up. When they spend money, they get a better sense of the fact that they are giving something up in return for something else.

Need something measured? The U.S. quarter measures exactly 1 inch in diameter.

When kids get to be 10 to 12 years old, however, it's time for them to move away from the jars and the piggy banks and learn more about how money works in the wider world and about the banking system. The age that kids are ready to make this transition is different for every child and every family. You'll know when it's time for your child because she will have a solid grasp of setting aside her earnings into the different savings and spending buckets and will be able to budget her spending effectively. She may begin to find the piggy bank cumbersome and that it takes too much time to track how much money is in there. At this point, it's time to move from the piggy bank (or the jar, can, or pillowcase) to a real bank account.

✓ THE BANKING SYSTEM

We discussed an overview of how the banking system ties into the overall economy in Chapter Three. The central banking systems in both Canada and the United States act as clearing houses to facilitate the transfer of financial liquidity amongst various enterprises and government units. Your local bank is tied into this central system in one of a variety of ways. Banks in both countries are regulated under federal law and all are tied into the federal deposit insurance plans: the CDIC in Canada and the FDIC in the United States.

When you first take your child to the bank to open an account, they may have several questions, depending on their prior knowledge and second-hand experience:

◉ *Can I get my money back whenever I want?*

When you're 11 and you've worked really hard cutting lawns, painting fences, and sweeping floors for the money you have earned, handing it over to a bank teller in exchange for a receipt or a new line in a bank book can be unsettling. Children often don't understand that banks are, for the most part, safe and secure. The trust that you place in the bank is secured by governmental regulatory law. Once you hand your money over to the bank teller, the bank is legally responsible for giving it back to you whenever you ask for it.

What happens if the bank gets robbed?

Even if kids believe their money to be safely tucked away inside the bank vault of your local bank, they might be worried about what happens to it if a bank robber runs away with all of the cash. Is it just lost?

Cash doesn't stay in the bank branch where you deposited it. There will always be some money held in the safe, but cash is mobile and travels from bank to bank. If a bank branch gets robbed, all of the deposited funds are covered by insurance and they are still available for withdrawal. Federal deposit insurance keeps people's faith in the banking system, without which, there would be 1930s-style mass runs on the banks.

Do I lose all my money if I lose my bank book?

This was one of my son's main concerns when he opened his first account. He was worried that if something happened to his bank book, his money would be gone. I explained to him that the book just records the transactions. His money is still safe. I also discussed with him why it is important to keep track of your bank book because unscrupulous people might be able to use it to withdraw your money. Each bank has different procedures for dealing with lost bank books, but most will issue you another one and place a note on the account in case someone else does try to use it. In some cases, the bank may close that account, open a new one for you, and transfer the money to ensure its security.

⑤ *What happens if the bank's money is destroyed in a fire?*

If the money in a bank branch is actually destroyed, for example, by fire, water, or other catastrophe, it is still insured. Destruction of currency is quite rare as funds kept in banks are locked in fire-proof safes. There is so much currency in circulation that the destruction of a small amount at a local branch will not significantly reduce the volume of the overall money supply and, thereby, increase the value of it.

> A dollar picked up in the road is more satisfaction to us than the 99 which we had to work for, and the money won at Faro or in the stock market snuggles into our hearts in the same way.
> ~Mark Twain

⑤ *How does the ATM machine across town get my money to give it to me?*

ATM machines are pretty cool to most kids even though they may be boring and annoying to us. You push a piece of plastic in and money magically materializes. It can be very difficult to make the link between their bank and bank account and the money that is dispensed from the machine. Try explaining it to your kids this way: the ATM machine is like a

It is illegal to burn or otherwise destroy currency in both Canada and the United States.

telephone operator. Its job is to connect various banking customers with their banks. So, for example, if you go to an ATM machine of a different bank than yours, it will still hook you up for a fee. The bank sends your banking information to the ATM machine and tells it how much money you have in your account. The ATM will allow you to withdraw based on what you have in the account and any maximum limits on withdrawals.

⑥ *What happens if I buy something with my debit card and I don't have enough money in my account to pay?*

Some kids' savings accounts have debit cards which allow them to purchase items as if they were credit cards. If a debit card is used to pay for a transaction directly, it may seem to a child as if the payment is accepted instantly without any confirmation that there's money in the account to back it up. In fact, most debit card and credit card transactions involve monitoring by the card company working with the bank. In the case of debit cards, transactions will be declined at the cash register if there is not enough money in the account unless the account holder has some type of overdraft protection. If your son or daughter is embarrassed at the checkout by his or her debit card being declined, you can bet that they will take budgeting and expense tracking more seriously in the future!

> Lack of money is the root of all evil.
> ~George Bernard Shaw

How come I'm making so little in interest on my savings account?

The days of double-digit interest on savings accounts are long past and there's no sign that they'll be returning any time again soon. Most checking accounts don't pay interest at all any more and savings account interest rates are often between 1 and 3 percent, hardly anything to write home about. When your children first start up their savings accounts, the interest can seem minuscule. Over time, however, not only will the savings continue to increase, but so will the interest, for two reasons. The first is that the interest is being calculated on increasingly larger balances. The second is that interest is also being calculated on the interest already paid. Depending on the account type your kids have, interest can be compounding monthly or annually.

None of our children has their own bank account. If they get birthday money, Mom and Dad hold onto it so it doesn't get spent on junk. We encourage them to set goals, and when they've saved enough, we go buy it together.

~ HEATHER M., COOPERSTOWN, NORTH DAKOTA

✓ BANK ACCOUNT OPTIONS FOR KIDS

While it may be easy to simply open bank accounts for your kids at your own bank, it pays to shop around, especially when it comes to kids' accounts. There are many options out there and each bank handles its "junior savers" differently. Some banks simply don't allow minor children to hold bank accounts. Some require that a parent's name must be on the account with the child. On the other end of the spectrum, there are banks that will give kids a checking account of their own, complete with checks and a debit card.

When comparing kids' bank account options, one of your biggest concerns should be fees. Banks in both Canada and the U.S. are somewhat regulated in the amount of fees they can charge, but they can still add up to be substantial. There may be account opening fees, monthly maintenance fees, debit card fees, check fees, electronic access fees, and many more. Some banks waive these fees on children's accounts. Be sure to read the fine print on the account before opening. Fees can take a big bite out of money that kids are trying to save.

Kids often start with a savings account to dip their toes into the banking world pool. Savings accounts are straightforward and easy to understand. As your children get older and get more money-wise, allowing them to open a checking account can help them become comfortable with electronic transactions. A debit card makes it easy for kids to pay for purchases from their account without the ability or the temptation to go into debt.

One word of caution about savings accounts with long-term savings, such as college funds or car accounts. These accounts can accumulate significant amounts of money over time. I always recommend that parents be co-signers on the account and that withdrawals require the signature of both the parent and the child. Many kids go through stages in their childhood when they make rash decisions and may rationalize to themselves that buying a motorcycle now is better than saving up for college. While I don't believe you should micro-manage your children's money management, it is still your job to keep them safe from serious mistakes that could hurt them financially for years. Bottom line—shop around for the accounts that offer your kids the most features with the least amount of fees.

✓ WHAT TO LOOK FOR IN A KIDS SAVINGS ACCOUNT

When you are helping your child open his own savings account, there are several factors to consider. Each bank's account offerings will be different. The more interactive your child can be with his account and the less the amount he has to pay in fees every month, the more likely he will be to continue to be enthusiastic about saving money. Here's what to look for:

⊚ *The highest interest rate available.*

> Some banks have "high yield" savings accounts which pay a premium interest rate based on the amount deposited. For example, if your daughter has $500 or more in her account, she may qualify for a higher interest rate. A word of caution: some of these accounts

require a minimum balance in order to get these higher interest rates and there can be penalties, or fees, in some cases, if the balance drops below the required minimum balance, or the interest rate paid could be less.

When these accounts have no fees, they are usually worthwhile as the funds will not be restricted and can be withdrawn at any time. If the savings balance will be invested for a year or more, however, these accounts should be compared to locked-in investments, such as Guaranteed Investment Certificates or Certificates of Deposits. Locked-in investments often provide much better returns than an open savings account.

No fees based on number of transactions.

Many savings accounts charge extra fees if you go over a certain number of transactions in a month. Never choose an account that charges for "too many" deposits. Kids should be allowed to put any amount of money in their accounts as often as they like. Many accounts charge only for an excess of withdrawals or transfers. If your child's spending plan includes far fewer transactions than the maximum, the fee won't kick in, but it's a wise idea to monitor the account for a few months to make sure your child isn't attracting any unnecessary fees.

Both online and in-person access for free.

When I was a kid, there was no such thing as online account access. If you wanted to know what your banking

Checks (or cheques) have been in existence since the first century when merchants would send notes of instruction for their banks to release funds to other vendors. They were used by the Knights Templar in the 12th century to provide pilgrims access to funds. "Check" and "cheque"—from the French word—were used interchangeably across the world until the 20th century. The British realm chose to use "cheque" so as not to confuse the meaning with other uses of the word. The United States uses "check" today.

I haven't found a bank yet around here that lets kids have chequing accounts but I wanted them to get the experience. I made them a "chequebook" in a word processing program. Each page is three blank cheques. Both of my sons have an "account" at the bank of Mom. When they get money they want to save, they give it to me and I deposit it into a separate savings account in my name. When they want to make withdrawals, they have to write me a cheque for how much they want. I take the money out of the account and give it to them. I also make a month-end "bank statement" for each boy that shows all of the transactions for the month. They have to compare the statement to their own records and make sure that everything is accounted for. Every now and then, I slip in an incorrect entry to see if they are really reconciling their statements. Most of the time, they are.

~ JENNY F., SAULT STE. MARIE, ONTARIO

transactions were, you went to the bank and either had your passbook updated or received a print-out of recent transactions. Now, most major and even regional banks allow you to access your account information over the Internet 24/7. Some banks don't even have branches and everything is done virtually.

For a child's first bank account, it makes sense to allow them to access their account both ways: in-person and online. Online access gives kids instant gratification to see that their accounts are still there and growing.

In-person access reminds them of the physical "bricks and mortar" banking system that is the backbone of the country's financial system. In these days of increasing banking fees, many banks charge extra for in-person service at a teller. Some banks even charge for accessing your account online and downloading it to a program like Quicken. Choose an account that does not charge a fee regardless of the method of access.

> There are several ways in which to apportion the family income, all of them unsatisfactory.
> ~Robert Benchley

✓ PAYPAL STUDENT ACCOUNTS

Parents in the U.S. have another option for helping kids with their first bank accounts. Children 13 and over can have a PayPal Student Account, which is tied to their parents' PayPal account. It is not yet available in Canada—but I continue to lobby for it!

PayPal—for those parents who haven't used it yet—is an online payment facilitator that allows subscribers to maintain a cash balance, have optional access to credit, receive payments from anyone with a credit card, even if they don't have a PayPal account, and make payments with an ATM card just like they would with any other bank card.

The PayPal Student Account went live in 2009 and allows PayPal subscribers with teenagers to open an account for the teen (which is really a sub-account of the parent) and to be able to set controls and monitor the activity.

How does a PayPal Student Account work?

A PayPal Student Account can be set up by a parent for their teen. It is a separate account for many purposes but it is actually a sub-account of the parents' account. The parent can view balances and transactions in the Student Account and can initiate transfers back and forth. An ATM card is issued in the name of the student and he or she can use it to make online and in-store purchases. The student cards have a very low limit, however. They can take out $150 a day at the ATM or make $500 in purchases—much lower than a regular PayPal account.

The parent can optionally restrict the student account to disallow transfers in and out of the account other than to the parent. Without the restriction in place, the student can receive incoming payments from, for example, an online job.

PayPal Student Accounts do not have any access to credit so the teen can only spend what is in the account.

> We have profoundly forgotten everywhere that cash-payment is not the sole relation of human beings.
> ~Thomas Carlyle, Past and Present

What are the benefits of a PayPal Student Account?

There are many ways in which a parent can operate the Student Account to help their child learn about money and finance. Allowances can be easily transferred, either individually or on a recurring basis. Also, if your teen needs money in an emergency, you can immediately fund their PayPal account to help them out.

Many companies now have the option of paying employees and contractors through PayPal so your child can receive income from an after-school job or even a business venture through the account.

Transactions from any PayPal account (including Student Accounts) can be downloaded and entered into a budgeting and accounting program such as Quicken. Teaching a teen how to track and budget for expenses is an important first step in her financial independence.

How To Set Up a PayPal Student Account

Setting up a PayPal Student Account is easy and takes only a few minutes. Under the "Products and Services" link on your PayPal home page, choose "View All PayPal Products" and select "Student Account." There are several video presentations in this section that walk you through the entire process and they are worth spending about 15 minutes watching.

Once you are ready to set up the Student Account, input the required information, including the student's name, date of birth, and a password that you will assign to the account. Your teen can change the password later, but you will still have access to the account.

A bank book makes good reading —better than some novels.
~Harry Lauder

During the set-up process, you will be prompted to transfer money over to the account immediately. You do not have to take this step now but there will have to be funds in the account before the teen can use it. You can also set up a recurring transfer to the account in the case of, for example, a set weekly allowance. The funds can be transferred from your PayPal balance or from your alternate funding source, such as a connected bank account.

In order to begin using the account, the teen will have to go into his or her email account and retrieve the code. When this is entered into PayPal on the first login, it will not be required again.

There are some important safeguards to the PayPal Student Account that can give parents some comfort. There is a daily ATM withdrawal limit of $150 (versus $400 for regular PayPal accounts) and a spending limit of $500 versus $1,500 for regular accounts. This ensures that a teen is responsible for his own money but can't spend it in huge lump sums. This is helpful when a parent is funding living expenses for a semester at college, for example. There are very few fees for using this type of account so it's a great option to keep more money in your kids' account.

When the PayPal Student Account has been set up, a notification will appear that will tell you the date when the ATM card is to arrive by. It is approximately two weeks before it arrives, so make sure to set up the account long before the student needs to use it.

Setting up a PayPal Student Account can ease your children into healthy money management habits. And it can give you the peace of mind to know that you can guide them from a distance.

✓ INVESTING YOUR MONEY

Once children have a good grasp of how bank accounts and saving work, the next step is for them to learn a little bit about investing. That doesn't mean that your daughter needs to start trading penny stocks tomorrow. But a little investment savvy can help them find appropriate places to keep their long-term savings. Here are the basics of investing and how to help your kids learn about them:

Risk and Reward

This is one of the most basic premises of investing—the more risk the investor takes on, the more the potential reward. Investors need an incentive to take on a risky investment, so the interest rate or the potential gain has to be higher. Investments that are guaranteed or backed by other securities, such as government bonds and certificates, offer less of a reward because there is very little risk to the investor. To illustrate the concept to your children, offer them two choices. The first is that they can give you a dollar today and you will promise to give them back $1.25 at the end of the week. The second choice is that they give you the dollar and, at the end of the week, they will get back $2.00 or they will get back $0.00. They will have to decide whether to take the "bird in the hand" or take on more risk and potentially have a greater reward. Every child—and every investor—has a different tolerance for risk and they will use their own level to determine which investments are the best for them.

Time is Money

You've probably heard that phrase a thousand times in your life but, in the investing world, it really is true. The concept has been around for hundreds of years but was best described by Benjamin Franklin. What the time value of money means is that having money today is worth more than having the same amount of money later. For example, if you could get $100 today or $100 in a year, you would rather have the $100 now. However, if you could have $100 today or $105 in a year, you might consider the options to be the same. The $5 is the time premium for having to wait for the money. In that example, $105 is the future value of $100 at a 5 percent annual return.

The reason this concept is important when investing is that the longer you lock your money into an investment, the more of a premium you will need. That's why long-term bonds and certificates often pay a higher interest rate than shorter-term investments. This will become clearer to your kids when you sit down with them and talk about what they want to do with their longer-term savings. Show them their various options for the time frame that they can put the money away for. For example, if they are using the money for college in 10 years, have your kids look at 10-year savings bonds or notes. Most banks post their investment rates on their Web sites.

> In the old days a man who saved money was a miser; nowadays he's a wonder.
> ~Author Unknown

Investing and the Cost of Living

When my son was seven years old, his best friend lived not far from us and would come over to play and hang out on a regular basis. My son didn't have a bank account or any money of his own invested yet, but he had just had a conversation with me about the savings bonds my grandparents used to purchase for me when I was growing up. He tried to explain to his friend what a savings bond was and why it was a good thing. The friend looked horrified. He said, "Why would you spend money on that when you could buy more Beyblades?" (which were all the rage when my son was seven).

What my son's friend didn't understand is that an investment is different than an expense. When you invest money, you expect that you will get it back—plus more! We invest money to try to beat increases in the cost of living. The cost of living rises when the economy is in an inflationary period. When there is inflation, what we can buy for $100 today will cost us more in the future. If our incoming money doesn't increase, we will have less funds overall to pay for our increasing expenses. If we stash our money under the mattress, it can lose value because prices rise around it. Investing money is the best way to keep up with increases in the cost of living.

As of 2011, the U.S. Treasury holds over $16 billion in matured savings bonds that have been unclaimed.

◉ *The Stock Market*

There are several venues and products in which to invest. One is the stock market. If you have a pension from an employer, you may be a participant in the stock market without even knowing it. There isn't just one "stock market," there are many. They are clearinghouses for the purchase and sale of corporate shares and other equity instruments. In Canada, the most well-known stock exchange is the Toronto Stock Exchange (TSX). In the U.S., it's the New York Stock Exchange (NYSE). Traders come to these venues every day to buy and sell on behalf of their clients. Think of it like a huge Moroccan bazaar. Things get bought, things get sold, there's lots of yelling, and deals get negotiated. With stock exchanges, it's pieces of paper that get traded rather than geese and bolts of cloth and olive oil.

There is a huge range of risk in the stock market. Some stocks are reasonably secure. Their price may go up and down a bit every day but they pay their shareholders (owners) regular dividends. Dividends are payments that corporations pay to their owners from their net profits. These are often called "blue chip" stocks. Some stocks can vary wildly in price. They can be $4.00 one day, $12.50 the next, and $2.75 the day after that. These riskier stocks can pay off in the long run, but they can also be worthless in the long run. High-risk stocks are only appropriate for seasoned investors who have money to gamble and a long time horizon over which to recoup any losses in value.

Direct stock ownership is unlikely to form a part of your child's savings account, but understanding how the markets work is an important skill. There are many ways to help kids learn about the markets, but the best is to let them have a "virtual" trading account. There are several educational sites on the Internet that allow kids to choose their stock portfolio and track their performance. It does not have to be that elaborate, though. You can simply

> October: This is one of the peculiarly dangerous months to speculate in stocks in. The others are July, January, September, April, November, May, March, June, December, August and February.
> ~Mark Twain, Pudd'nhead Wilson's Calendar for 1894

allow your child to select stocks from the daily listings in the newspaper or other sources, and help them to read the daily closing price of the stock. Microsoft Excel, or another spreadsheet program, can be set up to calculate the change in price of the stock from day to day. Allow your children to choose stocks that they can relate to. They're much more likely to understand buying shares in Mattel than in IBM.

⑥ *Fixed Income Products*

Your children are more likely to have first-hand knowledge of fixed income investments like bonds or deposit certificates than of the equities markets. Fixed income products have guarantees of at least the return of the principal invested, for the most part. They are, as a group, less risky than equity investments like stocks, and fit well with savings goals that are 3 to 10 years in the future.

A bond is issued by a government, corporation, or other entity in order to raise funds to operate or expand. In exchange for investors purchasing the bonds, the issuer agrees to pay the investor a fixed rate of interest every year until the bond matures. After the bond is purchased by the original investor, he can turn around and sell it to someone else. The original issuer is then responsible for paying interest to the new owner. The price of the bond changes over time as interest rates change. For example, a $1,000 5-year bond is originally sold for that amount—its face value. It pays 6 percent interest annually, which is the market interest rate for such bonds. The rate is fixed in the bond contract and cannot be changed. However, if market interest rates go up to 7 percent a year later, a bond that pays 6 percent is not worth as much as a new one that pays 7 percent. Therefore, if the investor is going to sell the bond, he will have to sell it at a price less than $1,000 to make up for the poor interest rate.

When children are using CDs or GICs in their savings portfolio, trading these instruments is unlikely so the market price is generally irrelevant. If the certificate pays 6 percent annually, that is the interest your child will receive until the certificate matures, regardless of current interest rates. Buying a CD or GIC with your child is the best way to help them understand how they work.

Precious Metals

Gold and silver and a host of other metals are traded in organized markets also. There are a number of ways these metals are transacted. Physical blocks of the metals sometimes trade hands. Gold and silver coins are bought and sold. Certificates representing precious metals trade on exchanges. The price of metals such as gold and platinum likely will be a barrier to your child stocking up on bricks of them.

It can be fun, however, to have a few silver coins in the savings plan. Some silver coins represent an almost pure

The grooves on the edge of coins are called reeding. When coins were made of precious metals, it was a common illicit practice to shave the edges of the coin before spending it to keep some of the value. Merchants had to weigh coins to ensure that they were all there. When coins became machine-stamped, edges were reeded to stop the shaving. Even though coins are no longer made from precious metals, the reeding remains on some coins to assist vision-impaired people to differentiate the coins.

ounce of silver and are widely traded. In Canada, the silver Maple Leaf $5 coin and, in the U.S., the silver Eagle $1 coin are both one ounce of silver. The face values of the coins have nothing to do with their actual value. The value is the metal itself. At the time of this writing, silver is trading around $47 an ounce, and the silver coins can be purchased at your local coin shop and at some banks for around this value.

I was really nervous when my daughter told me she got a credit card her first year of university. It was one of those campus drives, where the company comes and signs everyone up, giving them gifts and "no interest for six months." But she's been really conscientious with it. She knows exactly how much she charges on it every month and makes sure she has the money set aside to pay the whole thing when the bill comes in. I think she's handling debt really well and she's building up her credit rating, which will be important for her when she buys a house.

~ JOAN T., SAN FRANCISCO, CALIFORNIA

✓ THE BASICS OF BORROWING

One of my grandmother's favorite sayings was "Never a borrower nor a lender be," from Shakespeare. It's a wonderful thought, but not a very practical one for most people. People often need to borrow money for large purchases, such as a house, a car, or higher education. Teaching your kids how to borrow responsibly is something that can save them thousands of dollars, a ruined credit rating, and lots of heartache in future years.

Children are not legally allowed to borrow money until they become adults and can sign contracts. But they should still learn the basics before they ever get in a position to borrow. If your children already have a reasonable grasp on how interest works when you save money, you can explain borrowing as being the flip side of the coin. Instead of "lending" money to the bank and earning interest on it, you are borrowing money from the bank (or other lender) and paying interest on it. When you are the borrower, you are signing an agreement saying that you will pay back the original amount of the loan and all interest owing on the debt based on the terms of the agreement. If you do not pay it back and breach the agreement, the lender can go to court to sue you or can seize some of your assets in order to pay off the debt. It is extremely important to abide by debt agreements.

In 2011, a recovery team discovered what is considered to be the oldest known shipwreck in the Caribbean off the coast of the Dominican Republic. The ship sank in the 1500s, not long after Christopher Columbus arrived in the Americas. Divers found a treasure trove of gold and silver stamped coins that could be worth millions of dollars.

One way to teach your kids the concept of borrowing is by giving them an advance on their allowance. For example, if your daughter is saving her allowance up to buy a bike but doesn't quite have all of the money yet, you might want to loan her the difference, which will be paid back through future allowance earned. If you take this route, formalize the process, even if it is only a few dollars you are "lending." Write up an agreement that states the amount of the loan, the terms of the repayment, and the interest rate. Even a small debt like this should incur interest so that children can see that debt costs money.

✓ CREDIT CARDS

Depending on who you talk to, credit cards are either the best invention ever or the path to financial ruin. They are neither; they are simply another form of borrowing. Credit cards are likely to be your child's first real-world experience with debt when they move away from home. Credit card companies have very effective marketing and advertising techniques to ensure that they snare young adults as soon as they're old enough to sign a contract.

> Money is neither my god nor my devil. It is a form of energy that tends to make us more of who we already are, whether it's greedy or loving.
> ~Dan Millman

In a perfect world (well, at least, my perfect world), there would be no need for credit cards at all. It is just as easy to use debit cards for most purchases. In the United States, you can even use your debit card as a credit card to make purchases online or over the telephone. Unfortunately, credit cards play a role in building a strong credit rating, which we'll talk more about in the next section. Teaching kids to use credit cards responsibly is better than teaching them not to use them at all. Give them the skills they need to manage credit card debt appropriately.

The first lesson that kids need to know is that a credit card is different than a debit, or ATM, card. To a child, both are simply pieces of plastic and handing both over to a checkout clerk results in being able to buy things. Help your children to understand that a debit card allows you to access money you already have, while a credit card allows you to borrow money that you do not have. If you take your kids with you to the store and use your credit card, follow through when the month-end bill comes in. Show them the line item on the statement and show them the balance due. Explain that you have to pay for that shopping trip when the bill comes in, otherwise, you will have to pay interest on the balance. Let your kids compare the rate of interest they are earning on their savings to the interest rate on the credit card. They will quickly conclude that carrying a balance on the card is very expensive and takes money out of the cardholder's pocket.

I've always been scared to look at my credit score. I knew it was going to be bad. I had a credit card in university and wasn't able to pay it back. I finally decided last year to bite the bullet and look at my score. It was much better than I expected. The credit card default is gone because that was over nine years ago. Since then, I've been very careful with handling debt and that reflects in my score. I'm kind of proud of it!

~FAY C., DENVER, COLORADO

✓ CREDIT REPORTS AND SCORES

Do you know what's on your credit report? Everyone should. Your credit report is used by potential and current lenders and others to determine whether you are likely to be able to pay your debts. Your credit report may also be used by landlords, insurance companies, and even employers. Defaulting on loans or being chronically late paying credit card bills can affect your credit report for many years. Actively managing your credit report is one of the most important financial tasks you will have in your adult life.

There are three main credit reporting agencies (also called credit bureaus): Equifax, TransUnion, and Experian in the U.S. In Canada, the two main bureaus are Equifax Canada and TransUnion Canada. Most banks and lenders report the status of the loans of their customers to these agencies on a regular basis. Your credit report may show different information for each of the three bureaus, depending on how often they update the report and whether there are any errors. In both Canada and the United States, you are allowed one free annual copy of your credit report. Reviewing your credit report at least annually is important to ensure that you know what's on it and that there are no errors. Errors on your credit report can result in negative financial consequences, such as getting turned down for a loan. You can purchase access to your report on a more frequent basis from each of the three agencies.

> A bank is a place that will lend you money if you can prove that you don't need it.
> ~Bob Hope

Your credit report will show your name, social insurance or security number, your address on file, and details of each loan or credit facility you have. The balance of the loan, the credit limit for any revolving debt, and your payment history are displayed. Payments over 30 days late are recorded even if you have since paid them up to date. If you have any more serious financial incidents, such as foreclosures, bankruptcies, or default judgments, they will be reported. Most negative credit entries will stay on your report for seven years, whether you have since rectified the problem or not. Bankruptcies will stay on your report for 10 years.

All of the information on your credit report is converted into an overall credit score, which is often the number used by lenders to determine if you will get a loan and how high your interest rate will be. Some lenders develop their own in-house credit score but most use the FICO score. FICO was developed by the Fair Isaac Company and is used and reported by all three major credit bureaus. Scores range from 300-850, with the median being around 723 in the United States and 720 in Canada. The actual scoring mechanism is proprietary information and not publicly released, but it is partially based on your payment history, your total debt, and how much debt you have versus the total you have access to. For example, if you have a credit card with a $5,000 limit and you have racked up a balance of $4,500, your score will be lower than if you have the same card and only have a balance of $600. Having access to credit that you are not using improves your score.

So why should we tell kids anything about credit reports? They can cause enough fear in grown adults who aren't sure what's on them, so why burden kids with the knowledge of them? The reason is simple. Your kids' credit report, that they will start building when they become adults, will affect many aspects of their life. It will determine the interest rate on their mortgage (or even whether they can get a mortgage), who they work for, and how much overall credit they will have access to. They need to understand that credit mistakes they make when they are 18 will follow them for many years. Managing credit responsibly right out of the gate will give them a solid financial foundation.

- Once kids have the basics of earning, saving, and spending down, it's time to transition them from the piggy bank to a bank account.

- There are many options available to set up accounts for children, but your own bank may not automatically be the best option. Comparison shop for accounts and assess their features and fees before making a final decision.

- Kids can learn about other investment options through stock market games. Understanding the basic tenet of investing of risk versus reward will help your kids choose investments in the future.

- Knowing how borrowing and credit cards work gives kids an edge when they first venture out into the world on their own.

- Your credit report follows you around your whole adult life. At a minimum, kids should know that credit mistakes made early on can still haunt them years later.

LYN'S STORY

We have a whole elaborate points system. The kids earn points for each household task or chore. The tasks are as minor as wiping a counter all the way up to laundry. Points are based on difficulty of the chores and each point equals one cent or 30 seconds of computer time. The kids can trade in the points for non-school-related computer time or money. Money trade-ins happen at the end of the week. If there is misbehavior, points get taken away. If the misdeed was done to a sibling, the points get taken away and given to that sibling. It works out really well for teaching household responsibility, money value, and respect. This is a system I came up with myself to condense our many systems at the time.

My kids don't have bank accounts, but those old enough do have PayPal Student Accounts. This way, they can only spend what's there. Since I run my business online, the majority of my money goes through my PayPal. So it's easy to transfer money over to the kids if necessary. I can also do so via GreenDot MoneyPaks if there ever was an emergency-type situation where they needed funds right away but were not in my presence.

My kids are pretty well-versed in money. They know how much the bills are, how to save when shopping, and so much more. Our family is very thrifty and very adamant about valuing people before material things. My kids could probably use some self-control when it comes to books and learning, though. But then again, that's what I'm glad they spend their money on.

My kids know almost everything about my finances. I let them watch me pay bills, see my balances, figure out the budget, and more. Some people may think this is too much stress for kids. But I disagree. They would be more stressed later in life if I didn't teach them about it. Better to worry a little now than all the time later because they don't know what they are doing.

One of my daughters gets paid to write articles for one of my Web sites and occasionally sells her writing services to other venues. She is also taking procedures to set up an animal sitting and walking service. Her Web site is about ready to go live and she is just about prepared on other avenues as well.

I will always let my kids stay with me, either permanently or temporarily. If they were just transitioning, I would not ask them to pay room and board because the less they'd have to pay me, the more they'd have to save for getting back on their feet. If it was a permanent situation, I'd only ask them to pay whatever extra costs were associated with them being there, as well as have them purchase their own meals and supplies.

We plan to pay for each of our kids to go to college but encourage them to do well in school so that they will get scholarships. If they get scholarships, they will just get a bigger weekly allowance from us out of what would have been the tuition fund. While working through college does offer important lessons, learning should be the main focus, if at all possible.

I let my kids take charge of what they spend. They know full well what happens if they spend it all and have nothing left until the next allowance time. The waiting can be hard if they want to have fun but have no funds to do so. I think it's best to give kids pointers and let them learn while doing. When kids are regulated too much, it only encourages them to rebel, which is not good when it comes to finances.

~ LYN L., AURORA, COLORADO

CHAPTER EIGHT

Lessons of the Lemonade Stand: Business Principles for Kids

✓ INTRODUCTION

Of all the financial topics that you can teach your children, they will likely be most interested in business. Once kids understand that, theoretically, you can make unlimited income in business and could even be famous like Microsoft's Bill Gates or Facebook's Mark Zuckerberg, it sounds like a pretty appealing direction to go in.

Learning about how businesses work helps kids in many ways, even if they never run a business of their own when they grow up. Business savvy requires planning and estimation skills, the ability to effectively interact with customers, suppliers, and employees, and solid accounting and math skills. All of these skills will be useful later in life whether your children start their own businesses or just work in one.

There are many ways that kids can get hands-on experience with the business world. It can be as simple as helping you with a one-time yard sale, setting up a lemonade stand, or, as they get older, running their own small business part time. Encouraging your child's entrepreneurial spirit will both broaden her horizons and fatten her bank account.

✓ WORKING IN THE FAMILY BUSINESS

If your family runs a business, chances are that your kids already have had lots of exposure to the business world. They will overhear your conversations about sales and marketing—and dealing with obnoxious customers. You may even have your kids working part time in the business.

If you haven't "hired" your kids yet, consider doing so. It gives them valuable business experience in a safe environment where you can supervise and guide them. My son started out in my accounting practice when he was about eight years old. His first job was to fold, stamp, and mail communications with clients. As he got a little older, he could go through shoe boxes (or sometimes refrigerator boxes) of client receipts and sort and organize them by expense type. In the beginning, it took me more time to show him how to do things than it would have if I had just done it myself. Over time, though, he became a very valuable team member and learned a lot along the way.

There are a couple of caveats to hiring your kids in your business. I'm not suggesting you formally hire them and put them on the payroll. That is fine for older kids but there are many child labor and tax laws that you will have to follow to do it the right way. In most jurisdictions, children under 12 cannot be legally employed. If they are older than that, the employer-employee relationship between you and your child has to be the same as with any other employee. They have to be able to prove that they did the work (through time cards or other means) and you have to pay them a reasonable wage. As an example, you cannot pay your 13-year-old son $50,000 a year to do some filing after school. Tax authorities will see that as a ploy to transfer some of your taxable income to a child, who will pay less tax on it. Negative tax consequences can ensue. If you do want to formalize employment with your child, check the labor laws in your area and consult with a professional accountant before doing so.

You can, however, have your children help out in the family business without putting them on the books. The goal is to give them some real-world experience in the business world. Find tasks that they can handle safely and rotate them frequently to give kids the widest possible exposure. Talk to them about things that are going on in the business, such as why that customer who just left was irate, and why last month's financial statements make you very happy.

✓ PREPARING A RESUME

Whether your children end up working for a business or owning one, they will need to have a resume, a CV, or a bio of some description. Kids can put together their resume as soon as they've had their first job or taken their first training course. For example, if your daughter wants to set up a babysitting service, she would put her former experience and any child care courses she has taken on it.

There are easy ways to put together a resume—your child doesn't have to do it from scratch. Microsoft Word and other word processing programs have resume templates to choose from that already have the structure and format in place, and all your child has to do is to change the information presented. While you're helping your kids to prepare their resumes, consider how up-to-date your own is. It's always wise to have a current resume to remind you what skills you have and in what areas you may need more experience or training. An up-to-date resume also allows you to take advantage of sudden job or business opportunities.

My wife and I run a home-based lawn care company. All three of our kids grew up in the business and started working for us when they were old enough to lick a stamp or clean equipment. Our daughter now works for us part time while she takes business and accounting at university and our two sons still work on the weekends. No matter what they decide to do with their lives later on, I think it has been a great experience for them. They have learned how small businesses are run, how to deal with customers, and how to earn and budget their own money.

~ STEVE T., VICTORIA, BRITISH COLUMBIA

✓ HOW WILL YOUR KIDS MAKE MONEY?

If you have decided to encourage your children to start their own micro-businesses rather than working in yours, the first thing that you will have to figure out as a family is what product they will sell or what service they will offer. While they should always take the lead in coming up with ideas for businesses, it will be your job to oversee the planning process and make sure that:

In the United States, the highest denominated bill in circulation is the $100 bill, but, at one time, there were $500, $1,000, $5,000, $10,000, and $100,000 bills. In Canada, the $100 bill is also the largest, however, at one time, $500 and $1,000 bills were also legal tender.

1. they have considered all of the logistical considerations of the proposed business. (Will they need a cold place to store a case of lemons? Will they need to set up a petty cash box?)

2. they are setting up work that they can physically do safely.

3. they have thought through how much time it will take to work the business properly.

An example of the third is when my daughter, at around age nine, decided that she would make teddy bears by hand and sell them at the farmer's market. I had to help her change her entrepreneurial goals because we would have needed to build an addition to the house to set up storage space for all of the materials and stuffing. On top of that, each bear took her approximately 5 hours to make and she planned on selling them for $6 each. Also, it would not have been safe for her at that age to run a booth at the market without adult supervision. She ended up doing sewing projects for her friends at school from which she made a tidy profit, once she learned pricing.

Once you have all made a preliminary plan for a start-up business, it's time to formalize the planning process.

✓ THE UBIQUITOUS BUSINESS PLAN

Any business—even ones run by children—needs to start with a business plan. The business plan forces a budding entrepreneur to think through all the pieces that have to go together to make a business successful. It is a way of forcing someone considering opening a business to run through the numbers, think through the marketing and promotion plan, and formalize the budget for the business. Just like personal budgets are important for a household, a budget for a business is critical to ensure that it can continue to grow and thrive.

If your children are planning to start their own business, help them walk through the business planning process first to ensure that they have thought it through well. There is a business plan template at the end of this chapter to get you started.

Both of my children work for their own spending money. My oldest (17) does lawn care for neighbors while he looks for a "real" job. There don't seem to be any in our town. My younger son at 13 works on a farm with his dad. They buy their own items such as computers, game consoles, TVs in their rooms, and anything they want that isn't in my budget. I want them to know that while it's nice to have the things you want, you have to work for them.

~ SASS A., LOUISA, VA

✓ PROFITABILITY

The first issue that your child must consider when planning to start a business is profitability. Can they make any money doing what they want to do? For example, if they are going to make and sell knitted caps and scarves for babies, how long will it take them to do it, how much will the materials cost, and how much will they charge for it?

Part of putting together a business plan is to craft a budget or projection for at least the next 12 months so that the entrepreneur can see whether the numbers will actually result in a net profit or not. Preparing a projection can show holes in the plan and places where revenues need to increase or expenses need to decrease.

> Business is the art of extracting money from another man's pocket without resorting to violence.
> ~Max Amsterdam

Kids who are thinking about their first foray into the business world often forget to take into account all the costs of the venture. They focus instead on the revenues and mistakenly think that's the amount they can save from their business. Have your kids list out all the things they will have to spend money on in their business, such as advertising, raw materials, supplies, transportation, or meals. These estimates can go into the projection portion of the business plan.

At the end of the business plan, I have also included a section for them to figure their profit versus the time they have spent working in the business. This is a critical concept for every business owner to understand. In my accounting practice, I have seen new business owners (and even established ones) working for less than minimum wage, on the premise that they're saving money over hiring someone. What they are doing in reality is propping up a failing business model that wouldn't be able to survive if it had to properly pay for the labor it required to run it. The main purpose of a business is to provide the owner with a return on her investment (the money she has put into the business) and an income to adequately compensate her for the time she works in the business. Near the end of this chapter, I have reprinted an article I previously wrote that discusses the different hats a business owner wears and the need for appropriate returns for each. Older children will be able to understand its basic concepts and it is also a great refresher for you as the parent of an entrepreneur.

> Women prefer men who have something tender about them—especially the legal kind.
> —Kay Ingram

✓ ATTRACTING CUSTOMERS

Once kids know what they want to sell, they have to figure out who they want to sell it to. It's easy to think that customers will simply drop into your lap once you put out your shingle or make up some flyers. However, getting customers to buy from you rather than your competitor can be one of the most difficult tasks of small business owners.

Let's say your fifteen-year-old son is going to sell screen-printed T-shirts on the Internet. He has set up a Web site (because if he's anything like my son, he'll know far more about technical stuff than you will!). Customers can go to the site and order directly. Orders are shipped to customers the day after payment is received. Sounds simple, but how does your son get those customers there in the first place? He has to advertise and promote, and those are things that rarely happen overnight. He needs to get his message and links to the website in front of people who are in the market to purchase T-shirts. There are many ways to do that. Eventually, the site will be indexed by the major search engines and people will start finding the site when they search for certain keywords. It takes more than that, though. He can post information in forums he belongs to, work his social media contacts, and even set up a table at an event so that customers can see a sampling of what he's offering. Setting up a marketing and promotion plan is an important piece of the overall business plan.

✓ FINANCIAL STATEMENTS

While a business plan represents the paperwork that your budding entrepreneur will do upfront before starting the business, financial statements are the ongoing paperwork that he will do to record the transactions that happen in the business.

The age of your child and the complexity of the business will determine how formal the financial statements should be. If your six-year-old daughter sells lemonade at your yard sale on a Saturday morning, having her keep track of how many she sells and helping her calculate how much money she took in in total is likely sufficient. Older children should be tracking and calculating their costs as well, so that they can determine their net profit.

> When it is a question of money, everybody is of the same religion.
> ~Voltaire

If your child is older and has an ongoing business, she will have to learn some basic bookkeeping and accounting skills. It can be as simple as keeping track of everything in a manual ledger or computerized worksheet, or she can purchase an accounting program, like Quicken Home & Business, QuickBooks, or Simply Accounting. These programs will not only help record transactions but have reporting functions that will allow her to print off financial statements, which summarize financial results over time. These summaries can be compared to the original projections to see how on-track the business stayed and whether any adjustments need to be made to the projections. The following is a quick overview of financial statements reprinted from an article I wrote a few years ago:

Understanding Small Business Financial Statements

If you are like many small business owners, when you get a copy of your financial statements at the end of the year from your accountant, you flip through them, nod as if you know what they're trying to tell you, and file them away in a drawer, never to see the light of day again.

Knowing how to read your financial statements, however, can help you to understand what happened last year in your business and what's likely to happen this year. Let's have a look at the three major documents in a typical financial statement package.

The Balance Sheet

This is usually the first statement in your package. The purpose of the balance sheet is to give a snapshot of what your business owes and owns at a certain point in time. At the top of the statement will be an "As of…" date. This is the date (usually your business's year end) that the balance sheet reflects.

There are three main sections of your balance sheet. "Assets" (as you might suspect) list the types of assets that your company owns. "Liabilities" show you what your business owes—to the bank, to the government, and to others. The last section is called "Equity." This section shows you what your net interest is in the business. You'll notice that the total equity equals the assets minus the liabilities. Another way to view equity is that it is what would be left if you wound up the company and paid out all the liabilities with the assets.

One important note is how your balance sheet is valued. All of your financial statements are (with few exceptions) valued at the cost at wihich you made the original transaction at. For example, if your company purchased the building you operate in for $50,000 ten years ago and it is now worth $150,000, it will appear on your balance sheet at its original $50,000 cost minus depreciation. Your balance sheet is not a good indicator of the value of your business, only the historical transactions. There is great debate in the accounting community about whether historical cost is the correct valuation method (proponents suggest that it is, at least, the most objective method), but for our purposes here, it is sufficient to note that it is historical cost that appears on your financials.

> Empty pockets never held anyone back. Only empty heads and empty hearts can do that.
> ~Norman Vincent Peale

The assets and liabilities on your balance sheet are divided into "Current" and "Long Term." This is an important distinction and one that your banker will look at closely. It is important to have at least enough current assets to cover current liabilities.

The Income Statement

The second statement in your package is usually the income statement. At the top of this statement will be wording to the effect of, "For the period ended…" Where the balance sheet shows you a point-in-time snapshot, the income statement shows you your business's activities for a period of time, usually a year.

The first line or grouping of lines on the income statement shows you the revenues for the year. They may be called "Revenue" or "Sales" or "Gross Income," depending on the style of your statements. The revenue is the gross amount of income earned from your business activities, less the sales taxes. It is important to note that your sales will appear here even if you haven't collected the money yet. Financial statements are generally prepared using the accrual method, which places revenue and expenses into the period in which they are earned, not collected.

Following the revenue section is a listing of the expenses. You may find this list in alphabetical, size, or no particular order. My personal preference is to list them in alphabetical order to make it easier to locate a particular expense, but you may prefer another method, which is just fine.

Your revenue minus your expenses is called the "Net Income." This is the amount that the business will keep and add to the equity. At the bottom of the income statement, you may find a reconciliation of the equity. It will start with the income earned in the current year, add the opening equity, and subtract any dividends paid out to the shareholders in the year. The ending equity will be the same equity number found on your balance sheet.

Cash Flow Statement

This is probably the least understood but most useful of all the financial statements. The purpose of the cash flow statement is to show you where the money went during the year.

There are two main classifications on the cash flow statement: sources of cash and uses of cash. Every transaction the business has entered into in the year has either been a source or use of cash. The main source of cash, of course, is your net income. Other common sources are collection of accounts receivable, loan proceeds, and incurring payables instead of paying cash. Common uses of cash are paying payables, paying down debt, and buying equipment or inventory.

At the end of your cash flow statement, your current cash balance shows. The statement has reconciled your opening cash to your closing cash.

Many small business owners ask me, "Where did all the money go?" This is the statement that shows them.

> To suppose as we all suppose, that we could be rich and not behave as the rich behave, is like supposing that we could drink all day and stay sober.
> ~Logan Pearsall Smith

Getting a deeper understanding of the inner workings of your business is critical to your success and being able to interpret your financial statements is a powerful tool in your knowledge toolkit.

✓ MONEY-MAKING IDEAS FOR TEENS & PRE-TEENS

There are lots of ways for your budding entrepreneurs to earn money. They may even come up with business ideas that you have never even contemplated. As long as the idea is well-thought-out and planned, let them run with it. The one intractable rule, however, is that they be safe. You don't want your eight-year-old daughter babysitting infants, for example, or your ten-year-old son chopping firewood. The business should be appropriate to their capabilities and age. Then, just help them with their business plan and watch them learn about capitalism first-hand!

① *Pet and House Sitting*

For kids who love animals, pet sitting is a great opportunity to both make some money and spend time with animals. Kids can charge by the time spent or per pet. This is a service that often develops by word of mouth, but flyers can also be made up and posted around town, especially at local veterinary offices. Older teens can offer full-scale house sitting services where they can stay overnight in the house.

② Tutoring

Even pre-teens can effectively tutor younger students after school or on weekends. If your child loves school and is sociable, helping younger children with homework is a great work opportunity. The tutoring can be done in your home or in the student's home, depending on transportation arrangements and taking into account safety concerns. Tutoring most often lasts for a set amount of time (such as an hour twice a week) and is charged for by session. Teenagers can mentor students in many ways, including using an instant messaging or video program over the Internet.

If you have a torn or damaged paper bill, the government will replace it for you as long as you have more than 51 percent of the original bill.

③ Gardening/Yard Work

Busy professionals and older homeowners often need help with weeding, raking and other garden and yard chores. Most of these are perfect for pre-teens and can command a high hourly rate. Older kids can do more intense or heavy work such as using electric hedge trimmers or saws to clear brush. Flyers tucked into neighborhood mailboxes are the best way to get a good response. Kids can also make signs to post on yards they are caring for with their name and number on it.

◎ *One-of-a-Kind Crafts*

Some kids have a penchant for arts and crafts and this can be developed into a micro-business. If your child likes to crochet, scrapbook, or paint, he or she can sell crafts either locally at flea markets or online. Managing a sales booth is great experience for young business owners and teaches lessons in marketing, pricing, and customer service. For teenagers with a love of art, design services can be offered to business clients for logos or Web sites.

Ⓢ *Parent Helper or Babysitter*

While some pre-teens may not be ready (or legally able) to babysit all on their own, those who want to babysit in the future can become a parent helper. The parent helper performs most of the tasks of a babysitter but with the parents present. This can take the burden from busy parents and allow the pre-teen to get valuable paid experience that will help them be a babysitter in the future. Most states allow teenagers 13 and up to babysit without a parent present. The community may also offer babysitting courses to teach potential sitters how to handle various situations. These courses are a great resource.

Money is like manure. You have to spread it around or it smells.
~J. Paul Getty

✓ A QUICK WORD ABOUT INCOME AND SALES TAXES

Kids who earn employment income or self-employment income may be required to file income tax returns much sooner than most other kids their age, depending on their jurisdiction. A child should always file an income tax return if any taxes or premiums have been withheld on her employment income. It will likely result in a refund if the income falls below the taxable minimum.

Children who have net self-employment income should also file. The income will likely fall below the minimum and, therefore, not be taxed. In Canada, minors are exempted from having to pay Canada Pension Plan (CPP) premiums. In the U.S., minors may be exempted from Social Security Tax and Medicare, based on age and the total amount of net profit earned.

Money is much more exciting than anything it buys.
~Mignon McLaughlin,
The Second Neurotic's Notebook, 1966

The tax benefits and dangers of taxing income in children's hands is beyond the scope of this book and should be discussed with your accountant.

Your child may be required to register for federal, provincial, or state sales taxes on all sales made. Check with your local tax office to find out the rules in your area.

The following is a reprinted article I wrote about entrepreneurship and the importance of paying yourself what you are worth.

✓ ENTREPRENEURS: PAY YOURSELF WHAT YOU'RE WORTH!

In the start-up years of a small business, the owner is generally concerned with some of the more urgent issues, such as whether he or she can bring in the revenues that were forecast, whether that new customer is going to place an order soon, and whether he or she can keep up doing all the tasks that need doing.

But there's another critical aspect of your business—you. As owner and manager of your business, your time and investment are valuable and worthy of compensation, even in the start-up years.

You wear many hats in your business but the two main ones are that of manager and investor. We'll look at each of these roles separately.

The Small Business Manager

This is the role you are most familiar with. You are in this role when you work IN your business. Some of the main management functions are: business planning, human resource management, supply management, and sales.

You could hire a manager to perform these functions for you, but most small business owners do it themselves out of financial necessity. Say, for the time being, that you will keep the manager job. How well does it pay?

Let's look at your situation. Fill in the following information:

    (A) Amount of income from your business
           that you were taxed on last year: _____

    (B) Number of hours you worked in your
           business last year: _____

    (C) A divided by B =   _____

Are you at least making minimum wage? If you're like most owner/managers, you are making between \$1 and \$3 per hour. Hardly a sustainable wage!

Why is it that small business owners are willing to put up with such a low hourly wage? Because they believe they are building something for the long term. The problem is that 80% of all businesses fail in the first five years, and 80% of the rest fail in the next five. Odds are, there will be no long term, especially for those businesses that fail to plan well.

> I'd like to live as a poor man with lots of money.
> ~Pablo Picasso

Time and time again, I see clients in my practice who slave away at their businesses ten and twelve hours (or more!) a day for years without getting paid. Any money they do make gets farmed back into the business to keep it going. The toll that this takes on the business owner's morale, health, and family is astronomical. How long would you work for someone else and not get paid? Not very long.

You must plan for your own compensation. Not enough money in the cash flows for that? That indicates a problem. It means you are under-capitalized. It also means that you are permanently chained to your business. You couldn't hire a manager for free, so you will have to continue to do it forever. Not very heartening!

How do you know how much you're worth as a manager? Look around your industry. Look at what your competitors are paying their managers. Look in the Help Wanted section of your local newspaper. What are the salaries being offered to managers in similar roles?

Once you have a sense of what you're worth to your business, put your pay in the cash projections and make it work. If you're in the start-up phase, you may have to borrow from a lending institution in order to cover your salary. The business must be able to cover the principal repayments on the debt as well as the interest. If it can't, you will need to look at new ways of attracting increased business.

When you have planned out your salary, PAY YOURSELF FIRST! This is critical. Like any other area of your life, if you leave yourself until last to get paid, there's a good chance you will run out of money before you get around to it. You will make sure all other suppliers get paid because they will pick up the phone and yell if they don't get paid. You have to treat yourself just like any other supplier—worthy of prompt payment.

> Wealth—any income that is at least one hundred dollars more a year than the income of one's wife's sister's husband.
> ~H.L. Mencken

✓ THE SMALL BUSINESS INVESTOR

You wear another hat in your business. You are an investor in your business. You have most likely invested personal resources (cash, equipment) into the company, and like any other investment, you should receive a financial return.

This has nothing to do with the hundreds of hours you spend working. This only relates to the financial resources you have expended.

Let's say that when you started your company, you took $5,000 out of your savings account for start-up costs. What else could you have done with that money?

- Invest it in the stock market
- Buy a bond
- Put a downpayment on investment real estate
- Loan it to another start-up company

What would have been the benefit of doing those things? If you had invested in the stock market, you might have income on your investment in the form of capital gains or dividends. A bond would have generated interest income. Real estate will provide capital gains and rental income. A loan to another company would generate interest. In all these cases, you would be making a financial return on your $5,000.

You didn't do any of those things, however. You invested in your own company. Was it a good investment decision? It is if you are making a return on that investment that is similar to other investments that carry similar levels of risk.

For example, when you invest your money in the stock market, you expect to be compensated for the risk that you won't get your money back out.

When you buy a bond, you bear the risk that the underlying bond issuer will not be able to repay the principal or the interest to the bondholders. The issuer needs to compensate the bondholders for that risk.

Investing in your own small business has risks, too. In general, you know that the money is illiquid. In other words, you cannot take it back whenever you want. It is needed for the operation of your company for a certain length of time. You also know that the small business failure rate is extremely high. These are risks that should be offset by financial return.

So, how much return should you receive on your investment? Probably more than a government guaranteed investment and less than a junk bond.

Your accountant will be able to help you navigate through the owner compensation issues and set up a system that gives you the maximum return with the minimum tax consequences.

The only real business experience my kids have had was when they ran a table at a yard sale we had last year. They got to sell their own toys and chose the prices themselves. My youngest daughter organized the table and my oldest ran the cash box. Sometimes they got upset if someone looked at something on the table and didn't buy it, but they got over that eventually. In the end, I think they made more than me!

~ CAROL G., SILVER SPRING, MARYLAND

SAMPLE BUSINESS PLAN

Note that this is a simplified plan for reasonably uncomplicated businesses. It's a good way to get kids to start looking at all aspects of their planned businesses without overwhelming them with detail.

I. Executive Summary

In one or two paragraphs, summarize the detailed information that you will be providing below. You may want to go through the other sections first and leave this one until last when you know what points you want to make. Think about the Executive Summary as your elevator pitch. You have a three-minute elevator ride with an important banker and you have a very short time to let him know what your business is about and why it's awesome.

II. General Business Description

Describe what your business is going to do and how it's going to be set up. Give an overview of who your customer base is going to be and how you will get them to buy. Talk about the goals and objectives of the business and why it is unique and will be successful. Describe why you are qualified to run this business and what background you have that will ensure its success.

III. Description of Products and Services

Here's where you will go into more detail about what it is your business is going to provide. Where will you buy or how will you make your products? What kind of services will you offer? What is the unit cost? Include any photos or drawings you may have of products. Discuss pricing plans. What will you sell at? Will you offer any volume or other discounts? What challenges will you face in selling your products or services? What are your plans to overcome them? Why is your product or service better than your competitors'?

IV. Operational Plan

In this section, discuss how you will sell your products and services. Where will they be offered? How often will you be selling? Will you have an online presence and how will online sales be handled? If you will be subcontracting out the work (i.e., hiring someone to help you out), outline the details of the arrangement here.

V. Promotion and Marketing

Your plans to promote and advertise your products and services go here. Whether you plan on producing flyers, business cards, or a Web site, talk about how many, how they will be distributed, and what they will cost. Discuss how you will get your products or services in front of your target market. How will you reach them and what will you say to convince them to buy?

VI. Upfront Expenses and Capital Required

Most businesses, even tiny ones, need some money put in before the business even starts. You may need to print up some flyers or buy tables or office equipment before you begin. Outline any money that you will need before starting up and your plan for obtaining that money. For example, if you need $50 for start-up costs, and that money is coming out of your savings account, detail that out and also your plan for repaying the "start-up loan" back into your savings account.

VII. 12-Month Financial Projections

Following is a template to project out your expected revenues and expenses for the 12 months after you start your business. I have included some common expenses, but have left some blank spaces for you to fill in any that are not included here.

MONTH

	1	2	3	4	5	6	7	8	9	10	11	12	Totals
REVENUES													
Sales													
Other													
A. TOTAL REVENUES													
EXPENSES													
Advertising													
Materials													
Supplies													
Office expenses													
Miscellaneous expenses													
Other													
Other													
B. TOTAL EXPENSES													
C. NET PROFIT (A-B)													
D. # Hours Worked													
Hourly Earnings (C/D)													

✓ SUMMARY

- Kids can get real-world business experience either through working in the family business or starting one of their own, based on their interests and talents.

- If your children decide to start a micro-business, they will have to plan and document the financial results just like any other entrepreneur.

- Understanding financial statements helps your young entrepreneur know whether the business is financially on-track.

- There are many opportunities for business start-ups for minors. It is your job to make sure that the business idea is sound and safe for your child to do.

- There may be sales tax or income tax implications when children earn income either working for you or running their own business. Always check with your tax accountant while still in the planning stages.

JEREMY'S STORY

My wife died when our daughter was three and a half and it changed my world completely and all of the plans we had made for our little girl. We didn't have any life insurance. It was always on the "to-do" list but we just never got around to it with a small child running around all the time. I had to take on a second job just to keep the house and provide some stability in my daughter's life.

Looking back in hindsight, I should have been more open with my daughter about our finances and how I was budgeting. Most days, though, it was enough of a struggle just to put food on the table and keep the lights turned on. And she had enough pain and stress in her life. She had lost her mother. I didn't want her to have to worry about losing our home, too.

She's 19 now and in university in Toronto, taking law. I can pay for her schooling now that things are better for me financially. She has a good sense of money management and she must have absorbed some of it from our life together. I think mostly I'm just lucky to have a daughter full of common sense.

When she was about eight, she asked me to set up a bank account for her. She had been saving money in an old peanut butter jar but wanted something a little more official-looking. From the minute she had that bank book in her hand, she planned her savings. When she did get gift money from her grandparents, it was almost impossible to get her to spend any of it. She was addicted to seeing that bank balance grow. She housesat, pulled weeds, delivered newspapers, and did a host of other jobs to boost her savings. When she was ready to go to university, she was excited that she had enough money saved for the first two years of tuition and living expenses. My graduation gift to her was to tell her that I would be paying for all of her university expenses. She could spend her money on a new car or anything else she wanted. After two years of university, that money is still in her account. I'm very proud of her!

~ JEREMY G., KELOWNA, BRITISH COLUMBIA

CHAPTER NINE

A Little Off the Top: All About the Taxman

✓ INTRODUCTION

As adults, we spend a good portion of our working life doing so in order to pay taxes. We are taxed on our wages or other sources of income when we work and we are taxed when we buy goods and services. Depending where you live, you may be taxed when you win the lottery or even when you die!

Taxes are not something that most adults enjoy paying and certainly do not enjoy calculating and remitting at tax time. It is likely that the only things that your children have heard about taxes are that they are too high and other negative things that they may have overheard you say about them.

Kids will grow up to be tax-paying adults when they start working. Even as kids, they are paying sales tax on many of the toys, games, and other purchases they make. To be truly money-savvy, kids

"To pay through the nose" came from 9th century Ireland where the ruling Danes would cut the nose of those who refused to pay or were late in paying the Danish poll tax.

need to have at least a general understanding of what taxes are and why we pay them.

✓ WHY KIDS NEED TO KNOW ABOUT TAXES

Overall, taxes can take up over 50 percent of our total income for the year, between income, sales, and ad valorem or property taxes. Taxes are a significant part of our lives and how we manage our tax burden has a large impact on preserving our wealth over time. The earlier kids understand what taxes are and how to minimize them, the more of their own money they will be able to keep in their pockets over their lifetime.

It's also important that kids understand the role of taxes in our society. Without them, we would have no social services or national infrastructure. There are many adults who would like to pay no taxes at all, but probably wouldn't like the society we would have to live in if that were the case.

I guess I don't really teach my kids anything about taxes because I really wouldn't know what to tell them. I take all my stuff to the tax place in the mall at year end and they handle it. I almost always get money back, so I guess they're doing a good job. But I wouldn't know how to teach my kids to not have to pay so much in taxes. I sure wish someone would teach me, too!

~ BEVERLY J., HOUSTON, TEXAS

✓ WHAT DO KIDS NEED TO KNOW ABOUT TAXES?

There are two ways to look at the taxes we pay: by the impact on us when we pay them and the benefit to us when we get to use them.

Most kids have no concept of income taxes until they prepare their own tax returns. This usually occurs when they start working for a living. The first time they get a paycheck from their part-time job at a fast food restaurant, for example, they will get their first shocking tax experience when the net amount of their check doesn't look anything like what they thought they were going to be paid.

> Inflation is taxation without legislation.
> ~Milton Friedman

Sales taxes are a little easier for most children to understand as they will get first-hand experience with them when they accompany you to the grocery store or the toy store. They should understand why we pay this type of consumption tax, who pays the bulk of it, and its purpose.

✓ INCOME TAXES

The easiest way to explain income taxes to your children is by showing them your tax return. Explain that all individuals and companies have to calculate their income tax responsibility and remit it to the government. If you work for an employer, taxes will be withheld from your paycheck to partially satisfy this responsibility. The government doesn't want to have to wait until the end of the year if you owe lots of tax. Also, if you have self-employment income, you may have to remit it more often than at the end of the year for the same reason.

In Canada, it is the Canada Revenue Agency (CRA) that is responsible for administering the taxation system and collecting taxes. In the United States, it is the Internal Revenue Service (IRS) that performs the same function. These agencies have significant powers to enforce the payment of taxes. So it is always a good idea to file your tax return on time!

In Canada and the U.S., income taxes are levied at both the federal and state or provincial level, with the exception of a few states in the U.S. In addition, the U.S. also has municipalities that levy their own income taxes. It can be confusing to keep them all straight. Canada makes it easier than the U.S. as taxpayers only have to file one tax return that has both federal and provincial taxes on it (except for Quebec). The federal government then gives each province its share of tax revenue. In the U.S., taxpayers have to file separate tax returns.

Intaxication: Euphoria at getting a refund from the IRS, which lasts until you realize it was your money to start with.
~From a Washington Post word contest

After each calendar year is over, tax returns have to be prepared to calculate how much is owed in total and how much has already been withheld during the year. In Canada, these taxes are due on April 30th of the following year. In the U.S., they are due on April 15th. There are some exceptions to both of these rules.

The tax returns are also a vehicle to administer government subsidies and credits, so even if you don't owe any tax, you may be able to get some money back. Also, if you have overpaid your taxes during the year, you will get a refund for the difference. While some people love getting a refund at the end of the year, it just means that you've already given the government too much. It would be better to adjust your tax situation so that you don't give them the money earlier than you have to.

> I don't like money, actually, but it quiets my nerves
> ~Joe Louis

✓ SALES TAXES

While income taxes tax our inputs into the economy by our labor, sales taxes tax what we take out of the economy through our consumption. Sales taxes are remitted by the buyer at the cash register when the purchase is made. The retailer then has the responsibility of tracking the total sales taxes collected and remitting them to the government.

In Canada, there are both federal and provincial sales taxes in most provinces. In some provinces, they have been combined into a single tax, called the Harmonized Sales Tax, or HST. The purpose of this change was to simplify the sales tax collection process. In the U.S., there is no federal retail sales tax. Sales taxes are collected by states, and, sometimes, municipalities. Most states have a sales tax, but there are currently five states that do not collect sales taxes.

People who buy more things (usually wealthier people) end up paying more sales tax than others simply because they buy more expensive items. Sales tax is calculated as a percentage of the price of an item. Certain items are exempt from any sales tax, depending on what jurisdiction you live in. Basics, like food and children's clothing, are often exempt from sales tax.

✓ PROPERTY TAXES

On the Canadian $5 and $10 bills, the flag flying over the Parliament Buildings is not the Maple Leaf, but the Red Ensign. The Red Ensign has never officially been the flag of Canada but it was popularly recognized prior to the introduction of the Maple Leaf in 1965.

Levying taxes on assets is one of the oldest forms of taxation in existence, occurring long before any kind of income or sales tax. It was originally considered to be one of the most "fair" forms of taxation as rich landowners paid significant taxes and those who did not own property did not pay much in taxes.

Today, it is most often only real property, such as land and buildings, that are taxed in this manner, rather than investments or other types of assets. Property taxes are levied annually in most places by municipal governments in order to pay for local services. Property taxes are also sometimes levied on vehicles, but most municipalities just charge a fixed plate or tag renewal fee.

Property taxes often form the largest portion of a city or county's revenue and they have significant powers to make you pay or you can lose the property if you have back taxes.

There can also be taxes levied on the transfer or sale of property but these are separate from annual property taxes.

It was really a shock for my son when he got his first "real" job. He didn't understand the difference between gross and net pay. He was furious that his boss had taken money out of his paycheck. He didn't have any idea about tax withholding or employment insurance premiums. He's finally figured it out and understands he'll get credit on his tax return for the taxes he's already paid. I don't think he's any happier about it, though.

~ MARION K., SUMMERSIDE, PEI

✓ WHERE DO OUR TAXES GO?

One of kids' first questions about taxes asks where all that money goes. What does the government do with it? Do they put it in their pockets? Kids (and many adults) need a good understanding of the need for, and the usage of, tax to eventually take a bit of the sting out of paying it.

> That money talks
> I'll not deny,
> I heard it once:
> It said, "Goodbye."
> ~Richard Armour

Regardless of which level of government levies the taxes, they are used to provide services—sometimes directly to individuals and sometimes to other agencies that serve individuals. Kids who already have a bit of knowledge about how government works know that we are the government. The government represents us and our needs and wishes, in theory. There are many social benefits that we wish to have that benefit a great number of people. Programs like public education, roads, unemployment and welfare benefits, and even jails. It would be practically impossible for small groups of people to get together and decide which services they need and how best to fund them. This is the purpose of government funding. Different governments use their revenues for different purposes based on their mandate.

How the government uses the revenues they get from taxpayers and how much each should pay are sources of much of the political debates and arguments your kids will hear on television and read in the newspapers. Take some opportunities to make these connections for your children. If you're watching the news together one evening and the topic of whether to cut funding to social programs comes up, for example, explain that they are arguing over whether they have taken in enough money from taxpayers to keep paying out as much as they do.

✓ BRINGING THE LESSON HOME

Younger children won't need as elaborate a discussion of government and taxation. They won't be able to absorb all of it, for one thing, and it's not concrete enough for them to connect the abstract concept of taxation to having to pay an extra $1.25 on the train set they just bought with their savings.

Help young kids "get" the concept of tax with a family scenario. Let's say everyone in your household wants to buy an ice cream maker. Everyone would use it and it certainly doesn't make sense for each of you to buy your own. That would be wasteful and cost too much money. And, even if each of you could buy your own, Mom is the only one who knows what kind is the best to buy and where to go buy it. Ask your children what they think the best way is to get an ice cream maker. They will likely come up with the answer that everyone should chip in to buy a single ice cream maker and that everyone should give the money to Mom and let her go and make the purchase because she knows what she's doing. That's the same concept as taxes. We all chip in for things we all need and desire in the country and we task the government with spending those funds appropriately.

✓ TAXES AND ALLOWANCE

Some parents choose to teach their kids about taxes by withholding a "tax" from their allowance. This money is often put away in a savings account and presented to the child when she goes off on her own. We have never done that with our kids simply because it only illustrates the "giving" part of taxes in the short term. I don't believe that there is a clear enough connection between taking the money and giving "benefits." However, it does work for some families, and you may wish to consider this family "tax."

My son is a Certified Public Accountant now so he has a good handle on income taxes. In fact, he does mine every year for me. I think kids should learn about taxes when they're younger but they should learn about more than just paying them. They need to understand that taxation is how the government gets its money to do all the things we want it to do, like build roads and provide services. It's the money that we invest in our society that we all benefit from.

~ JENNIFER B., CORNELIUS, OREGON

✓ WHEN DO KIDS HAVE TO START PAYING TAXES?

There are different criteria for when kids have to start filing tax returns and paying taxes based on:

- Where you live
- How much income the child has
- What type of income the child has (earned income like employment or self-employment versus passive income like interest or dividends)
- Whether taxes have already been withheld during the year

Even in many situations where a child has below the amount of income required to file or to pay taxes, there may be benefits to filing to get credits or to build the cumulative income upon which contributions can be made to tax-deferred retirement plans in the future. Always check your particular situation with your tax accountant.

The first year that my daughter had a job, I wouldn't let her take her taxes to an accountant. I made her sit at the kitchen table with me and do them by hand. I find that it's a really great way to show young adults how taxes work. She goes to an accountant now but she knows how to read her tax return and she even caught an error on it once. I think it's an important skill to have.

~ BERNIE M., THE PAS, MANITOBA

✓ SUMMARY

- Income, sales, and property taxes take a big bite out of our income and our wealth over time. Teaching kids about taxes early helps them to minimize them later in life.

- Taxes are not simply just an expense. We gain benefits from paying taxes such as hospitals, schools, roads, and police forces.

- Depending on where you live, taxes can be levied by federal, provincial or state, or municipal governments.

- Younger children can learn about taxes by simplifying the concept to the family level. Some families even take "taxes" out of kids' allowances.

- Check with your tax accountant once your child starts earning income to see when she has to start filing tax returns.

JO'S STORY

Our two girls earn a base pay for completing all of the chores assigned to them. Since they are at very different stages in maturity (one is 5 and the other is 10), the level of responsibility and the allowance amount are not the same. Both kids have clear guidelines about what is expected of them and know if they complete their tasks they will get paid. If they choose to slack on the responsibilities, they may be docked a portion of the allowance. The other side to that is that if they are caught "doing good" and going above and beyond their responsibilities to help out, we also reserve the right to pay a small bonus. This system works well for our kids because it's teaching them responsibility and how things work in the real world. If you don't complete the work, you don't get paid! One thing I found helpful when using this method with my 10-year-old is to actually draw up a responsibility contract with her. I created a simplified version of the type of contract I use for my freelance work. The contract spells out what she is and isn't expected to do to earn her allowance, as well as what my expectations are. (For instance, cleaning your room entails making sure all clothes and toys are off the floor and put away, the bed is made, dirty laundry is in the hamper, etc.)

When my kids go off to live on their own, I will tell them to stay away from the credit cards! Just because financial institutions are willing to give them to you, doesn't mean you can afford to pay them off. It took me years of hard work to get rid of debt that was accumulated by charging little bits here and there. By the time it was paid off, I couldn't even remember what I had spent the money on in the first place. Instead, try to save up for purchases. If you do get one credit card for emergency use, use it sparingly, and pay it off in a timely manner.

Since my kids are only 10 and 5, they don't make a lot of money on their own yet. My 10-year-old has earned money by dog-sitting for our friends a few times, though.

We are putting money aside to help with our kids' college educations. I think it's important for them to have time to devote to their studies and relationships. When I was a student, I spent so much time working that it was sometimes difficult to keep up and still find time to sleep. That being said, I do believe that kids should also pitch in to pay for some of their own education. When everything is handed to you, you often don't appreciate it as much as when you have a part in earning it. Of course, ideally, we'd love it if they'd both end up earning scholarships to help carry the costs of their education. Then maybe we could spend some of the money we've been saving to do something fun to reward them for all the hard work...or take a cruise!

Our kids are generally allowed to make decisions about how to spend their own allowance. We do try to guide them if we see them repeatedly wasting money on things that they won't really use. Money sometimes burns a hole in their pockets, and they want to spend it as soon as they get it. One way I help my 5-year-old with this is to keep a short list of items she expresses an interest in having, where we see them, and how much they cost. Then, when she gets money, I gently remind her of them. If they receive a larger monetary gift or earn extra money somehow, we do encourage them to save some of it or put it aside to buy a bigger item they've been wanting.

~ JO B., ORMOND BEACH, FLORIDA

CHAPTER TEN

Guarding the Castle: The Basics of Insurance

✓ INTRODUCTION

When I was growing up, I did not understand anything about insurance. I didn't know that if our house burned down, we would have the money to build a new one. I didn't know that if my mother died, there would still be enough money to live. I didn't know that, growing up in Canada, we could walk into a hospital and it was already paid for indirectly through our taxes. I didn't know any of those things until I lived on my own and discovered how important they were.

Insurance forms another critical foundation stone in financial stability. Not only do you have to build up your assets, you have to be able to protect them from harm, otherwise you run the risk of losing them. Many parents I've run across in my accounting practice are afraid to talk to their kids about insurance because it also involves discussions about death, illness, fires, and other scary potential events. They want to protect their children from these realities. However, NOT understanding that things will be okay if those calamities happen can scare children even more. Teaching them about this basic financial security can help them feel more secure at home and start them off on the right foot when they start building their own wealth.

✓ TYPES OF INSURANCE

At its most basic, insurance is simply a contract between the insurance company and the insured (you). It says that, if certain events occur, the policy will pay the insured or his family a certain amount of money to cover all or part of the loss. The main types of insurance that most individuals deal with are life insurance, health insurance, and property and casualty insurance. Businesses also need different types of business insurance. Depending on the types of assets you own, you may have other kinds of specialty insurance. We'll look at the basics of each one and then discuss ways to share the information with your kids.

✓ LIFE INSURANCE

No one wants to think about dying or have to imagine what their family's life will be like when they're dead. Having enough life insurance in place, however, is a critical component of anyone's financial planning and is especially important for parents with minor children as future expenses are often higher, including college.

> It is better to have a permanent income than to be fascinating.
> ~Oscar Wilde

These are the three major categories of life insurance:

Term life—this is straight-up, plain vanilla insurance coverage without the frills. As per its name, term life insurance is in force for a set term, often 1 year or 5 years, during which time, the premium and death benefit is fixed. When the term is up, the insurance renews, but the premium will likely be higher as the policyholder is older and statistically at a greater risk of death. Upon death, the face value of the policy is paid to the beneficiary.

Whole life—this is a life insurance type that contains both an insurance component and a savings component. The premiums cover both the face value of the policy and an investment account. The policy builds cash value over time and the policyholder can borrow against it or get it back on surrendering the policy. The premiums are fixed for the entire length of the policy and the death benefit never changes. Insurance agents love to push whole life as the commissions are higher than with term life. However, the major downside to this type of policy is that the policyholder has no control over the investing portion. The investment strategy is determined by the insurance company.

Universal life—this is a fairly new insurance product on the scene. Universal life takes a whole life policy and makes it more flexible. It increases both the potential risks and rewards. There is still a savings component to it that cannot be controlled by the policyholder. The premiums and death benefits can both change based on actuarial experience and investment returns. While U-Life can often be used as a sophisticated tax planning

In late 2011, Canada will join over 30 other countries in switching from the traditional cotton-based paper money to plastic bills. The plastic money is expected to last two and a half times longer than paper and resist crinkling, thereby making it easier for vending machines to handle. It will also be fully recyclable at the end of its life.

tool for high income taxpayers, it is rarely the right type of policy for small business owners and entrepreneurs.

Determining how much life insurance you need is an art, not a science. Regardless of what the insurance agent is going to calculate for you (which is often far more than you would ever need), there are five main things to take into consideration when choosing a face value for a life policy: burial, debt, income replacement, future needs, and estate planning.

The first one considers the cost of your funeral. Unless you want your family to pay for your funeral from their savings, this is the absolute minimum amount that you should be insured for. Depending on your preferred method of disposal, a traditional funeral can cost $10,000 or more, much higher in big cities.

The second component of your family's financial needs post-death is debt. Start your family off with no debt after you die to minimize their income needs. List out all of your debt, including mortgage, credit cards, car loans, and other consumer debt. Include this total in the face value of your policy. As you pay these debts down over time, more of the policy value can go to increasing your family's wealth.

Third, look at what your income pays for now other than debt. Even if your family is debt-free after you die, they will be faced with everyday expenses such as groceries, day care fees, utilities, and entertainment. Your spouse may continue to work after your death but, if you have small children, your spouse may not be able to work as much as he or she did before due to new child care responsibilities. Include an amount in your coverage to pay basic ongoing expenses for at least a few years.

The next thing you need to examine is future income needs. Big-ticket items like college tuition, weddings, and vacations will be a financial burden to your significant other when you are gone. Include some of these items in the face value of your policy.

Finally, you should discuss your will and your estate planning needs with an experienced lawyer or financial planner. There may be tax implications in transferring assets to your beneficiaries, and life insurance can be an important tool to ensure that the tax burden can be met.

Beware of insurance agents who play on your generosity and love for your family. Coming from an insurance background, I have seen this time and again. If you hear questions like, "How much do you think your family deserves if you die?" or "How much money would send them the message that you really loved them?", run the other way. Do your calculations first and walk into the meeting knowing how much insurance you need.

Being a life insurance agent, I always thought my kids understood what insurance was. I guess I figured they would just pick it up over time. When we had to have our car replaced after an accident, I realized the kids really didn't know much about how insurance works and why it's an important part of a financial plan. My son is off at college now and has his own policies. He's pretty good at knowing how much insurance he needs.

~ JANET F., ATLANTA, GEORGIA

✓ CHILD LIFE INSURANCE

When talking to your kids about life insurance, a question that is likely to arise is whether you have insurance taken out on their lives. Each family has to decide whether child life insurance makes sense for them or not, but there are many good reasons to forego it. The most important message of the conversation, however, should be that, if you don't have child life insurance, it doesn't mean that you don't love your kids. And you need to remember that, when you sit down with your life insurance agent to go over your insurance needs. The question of child life insurance will invariably arise. It can be a very emotional conversation as no one likes to contemplate the death of their children. Unfortunately, there are some unscrupulous life insurance agents out there who play on this emotion and sign you up for insurance you do not need. When I review personal finance issues with my clients, I often find that they are paying premiums for life insurance on their children that costs them money every month and is unnecessary. I often help them cancel the policies and direct those premiums into a college fund instead.

> Put not your trust in money, but put your money in trust.
> ~Oliver Wendell Holmes, The Autocrat of the Breakfast-Table, 1857

Life insurance serves three basic purposes: to pay out your debts on your death so that your beneficiaries will not inherit them; to replace your income so that your family does not have to lower their standard of living; and to pay any estate taxes required when you die rather than your beneficiaries having to sell some of your assets to pay the tax.

None of these situations occurs when a child dies. In most situations (unless your child is a famous actor), your child is not responsible for bringing income into the house and does not own any taxable assets. From a purely financial perspective, a child's death means a reduction in expenses going forward. Therefore, the main purposes of life insurance are not required on a child's life.

There is one main expense that you will have if your child dies: the funeral. A child's funeral can cost anywhere from $5,000 to $10,000. If you do not have other sources of funds to cover this expense, you may wish to take out a term life policy with a $10,000 face value. The premiums on a small policy like this will be minimal and the policy can be transferred to the child when he or she becomes an adult.

Your life insurance agent may try to sell you on the savings feature of a whole life policy on your child. Whole life insurance has a basic insurance component and an investment component. The premiums are higher because some of it goes to the investment pool. Depending on the terms of the policy, you can borrow against the investment component in the future. Your agent may advise you that it is an inexpensive source of college funds. However, there are many downsides to a whole life policy. You have no control over the investment side at all or the returns that it will bring. The investment goals may not match yours. As an alternative, you could take the difference in premium between a whole life and a term (straight insurance) policy, and invest it in a college fund directly for your child.

It can be difficult to remain practical and unemotional when deciding whether to insure your child's life. Insure the costs that you cannot afford and invest in your child's future on your own.

✓ HEALTH INSURANCE

Health insurance is one of the most confusing decisions that any person has to make. Canadians have it much easier than Americans in this respect because they have universal health care paid through taxes. This means that anyone can see a doctor or go to a hospital without having to pay. There are exceptions to this and some procedures are not covered. One such example is out-of-country coverage if you go on a trip and have to be medically treated in another country. Separate insurance is required for this possibility. As such, the rest of this health insurance section is dedicated mostly to American parents.

Health insurance coverage varies greatly from company to company and policy to policy. Some health insurance plans cover everything from regular preventative visits to the doctor to major medical crises. Some policies require a co-payment on all money paid out. Most have a deductible. They all have one thing in common—they are expensive. It's enough to make anyone want to just ignore it and not bother. However, you will do so at your own peril. Medical bills are the number one cause of both mortgage foreclosures and personal bankruptcies. No one ever thinks they will get sick enough not to be able to work or end up in a hospital bed for weeks on end at $10,000 a day. It could happen to anyone. It could happen to you. Here are the basics of how health insurance works:

Coverage—this is the list of medical situations that the policy will cover. If the policy includes routine visits to the doctor and annual preventative screenings, such as prostate exams or mammograms, the premiums will be substantially higher than for a policy that covers only hospital admissions. Some policies will specifically exempt certain conditions from coverage. The major exemption in most policies is pre-existing conditions. For example, let's say that you have had a doctor confirm that you have lupus. You decide it's time to get health insurance but you don't want to reveal to the insurance company that you have the disease. If, down the road, the insurance company can prove that you lied on the application about this pre-existing condition, they can deny any pay-outs related to it. You don't want to find out in a few years that you have been paying premiums but have no coverage for your most major health issue.

Other policies can exempt specific (expensive) conditions such as cancer or multiple sclerosis. Always read the fine print before signing on to any health insurance policy.

> He is rich or poor according to what he is, not according to what he has.
> ~Henry Ward Beecher

Co-payments—this is the amount that the insurance company expects you to pay as your share of the medical expenses. A common split is 80/20, meaning that they will pay 80 percent of a covered expense but you have to pay the remaining 20 percent. The higher the co-pay amount, the more money has to come out of your pocket every time you try to use your insurance. Higher co-pays will reduce your health insurance premiums but, if you expect to make use of the policy frequently, it may end up costing you more in the long run.

Deductible—this is the amount of medical expenses you have to incur before the insurance company will pay anything at all. Let's say, for example, that you had a minor in-patient surgical procedure, with the total bill coming in at $12,500. If your health insurance policy has a deductible of $5,000 and a co-pay of 20 percent, you will have to pay all of the first $5,000 and 20 percent of the rest, for a total of $6,500. The insurance policy will pay the other $6,000. Higher deductibles mean lower premiums—but more out-of-pocket expense to you. When choosing a deductible amount for your policy, think about your financial resources. Do you have $5,000 in savings to pay the deductible or would it set you back financially? Choose a deductible that you have the financial resources to cover.

> I am having an out of money experience.
> ~ Author Unknown

One popular health insurance strategy for self-employed people who don't have unlimited resources to pay for Cadillac health insurance plans is a combination of catastrophic coverage and a Health Saving Account (HSA). Catastrophic coverage is simply a health insurance policy that only covers major medical situations like accidents and terminal or chronic illnesses.

Catastrophic coverage plans are often called high deductible health plans (HDHP) because the deductible amount is high due to routine procedures not being covered. The premiums for this type of plan are far less than more inclusive ones but still give a base level of protection against losing your house if you get sick or injured. You can couple such a plan with an HSA. An HSA is an account into which you deposit up to an annual maximum of $3,050 for individuals and $6,150 for couples filing jointly. The limits change annually so check the most current IRS information. You are only eligible to open an HSA if you have catastrophic coverage. The contributions are tax-deductible and, when used for medical expenses, the withdrawals are tax-free. This means, for example, that if you go in for your annual doctor exam that costs $120, you can pay for it with the funds in your HSA and the bill is tax-free. If you were to simply try to claim your uncovered medical expenses on your income taxes, you would only be able to get a deduction over 7.5 percent of your income.

An HSA is also a great way to save for retirement if you are already maxing out your IRA. If you withdraw funds from your HSA for non-medical purposes if you are 65 or older, there is no penalty on the withdrawal and you simply pay tax on the withdrawal. It's an opportunity to defer more tax until retirement than IRA limits allow.

> I tried once to explain life insurance to my 4-year-old. I thought she was understanding what I was saying when I told her that, if I died, we were insured. At the dinner table last night, she was excited to share with Daddy her newfound knowledge. She proudly exclaimed, "Mommy won't die 'cause we have essurance." She didn't understand that insurance can't bring people back from the dead. I will wait another few years to try to explain it again.
>
> ~ ANNIE J., FLINT, MICHIGAN

✓ PROPERTY & CASUALTY INSURANCE

Property and casualty insurance protects your hard assets, such as your home, your car, your boat, or your cottage. It also often covers damage caused by your property to someone else's property. If your car gets into an accident or your house burns down, this is the type of insurance that will cover it.

> "If you pay peanuts, you get monkeys."
> ~James Goldsmith

Property insurance also covers injury to others on your property. For example, if someone came to visit and slipped on ice on your front porch, your insurance would cover medical and other costs. Each policy is different in its coverages, so know what you are being insured for and what's not covered.

Like any other type of insurance policy, there are often restrictions on what property insurance will cover. Some home insurance policies cover wind damage from hurricanes and some do not—especially in hurricane-prone areas. However, no policy covers water damage from hurricane flooding, which causes most of the damage. We have most recently seen the impact of this in the wake of Hurricane Katrina. Those who did not have supplementary flood insurance policies were not compensated for the loss of their homes, a big reason why some houses in New Orleans still stand ruined and empty today. Consider a flood insurance policy on top of your homeowners' policy if you live in an area prone to storm flooding.

Damage caused by lack of maintenance also isn't covered under most policies. There are many detrimental things that can happen to a home when it is not kept up properly. Without pest control, termites can take up residence and destabilize the structure of your home. A neglected roof allows the sheeting underneath to rot and cause dampness in the attic. A leaking pipe can allow mold to grow between the walls and in the drywall. All of these can be expensive to fix but none of them is covered under your homeowners' policy. Policies assume that you are regularly maintaining the property.

Because your home is one of the largest assets you are likely to own, it's incredibly important to make sure that your policy covers what you think it does. And, if you run a business in your home, you will likely also have to get a policy rider to include the business portion of your home.

✓ BUSINESS INSURANCE

There are several types of insurance policies that get lumped under the name "business insurance" but, in this section, we will discuss the main one: business interruption insurance. It is the coverage that is most likely to be overlooked by small businesses but one that can protect them in a catastrophe.

Business interruption insurance covers you financially if you can no longer do business because of a temporary occurrence such as damage to your home office or a hard-drive crash. Many home-based business owners believe that their property insurance will cover them if damage to their home halts their writing business. However, property insurance will only cover the damage to the property, not the loss of income because of the damage.

It is tempting to simply write this coverage off as unnecessary. If you wouldn't be able to work for a week or more if your home office (along with the rest of your house) burned down, investigate this type of policy with your insurance company. Most property and casualty insurance companies either offer this type of policy or partner with other companies who do.

I never had any life or health insurance until a good friend of mine died. She left her husband and kids with a huge mortgage and a mountain of debt. They had to sell their house and move into a small apartment because they couldn't afford it anymore without my friend's income. I was explaining this to my 14-year-old daughter one day. She said to me, "That can't happen to us, right?" Well, of course it could. I took care of our insurance the next day.

~ SARAH A., JACKSONVILLE, FLORIDA

✓ WHAT KIDS NEED TO KNOW ABOUT INSURANCE

Whew! Now that you're all up to speed on the basics of insurance, do your kids really need to know all that? Of course not. Older kids who are close to moving out on their own need more detail about the different options that insurance policies have and how they will fit into their lives. When kids first move out on their own, they need to have basic life, health, and contents or property insurance, and that is something that you, as a parent, are best equipped to help them with rather than leaving them vulnerable to persuasive sales pitches from insurance agents.

These are the main points that younger children need to know about insurance:

① You pay money every month (or at least on a regular basis) to have the right to have your losses paid for if something bad happens.

② You can insure your house, your car, your business, your health, or your life. Insurance does not bring any of those things back, but it compensates you financially for the money you lose because of the catastrophe.

③ You are the most important asset you own once you start working for a living. It is very critical to insure your lost income if you became disabled.

④ It is impossible to insure every single thing, but you can insure against most calamities.

✓ SUMMARY

- There are many types of insurance that kids will need as they grow up and move out on their own. Getting an early overview of the purpose and mechanics of insurance starts them off on the right foot.

- One common misconception that young kids especially can have is that insurance brings back the item (you, the car, the house, etc.) rather than just compensating for the financial loss.

- Canadians do not have to worry as much as Americans about health insurance since their health care is, for the most part, covered by universal health care. However, disability insurance is still an important consideration.

- Child life insurance is rarely necessary because there is no need to replace the income of the child.

- Younger children don't need to know all of the intricacies of the insurance industry, just a basic knowledge of what insurance does.

AMY'S STORY

I really wish I had taught my kids about money the right way when they were younger. I guess the problem was that I really didn't know anything myself and I didn't want to sound ignorant to my kids. They're all grown up now and I guess they've figured out that our money situation was a hot mess when they were little. My husband took off when we had two little kids. I found out three weeks later that I was pregnant again.

I remember one time when I was pregnant and my son was five and my daughter four. A truck pulled into the parking lot of our building. I knew even before he got out that he was there to shut our power off. I tried reasoning with him and tried to set up a payment plan, but his only job was to shut off the power. I will never forget the way he looked at me when I tried to talk to him. He dealt with deadbeats all day long. I was just another one. I will never in my life forget that look or the shame I felt trying to get him not to turn off that switch.

It's a little easier for us now. I have a decent job with some benefits and a pension plan. I can even sock a little money away in an RRSP. My son is fifteen now and getting ready to get a job of his own. I want to make sure he doesn't make the same mistakes I did and have to fight so hard. I don't ever want someone from the power company to look at him like he was a deadbeat. I try to teach both my kids to budget now and to always make sure they have some money tucked away in case they need it some day. I try to tell them that they can't spend it all every time they have it in case a time comes when they don't have it. I hope they listen.

~ AMY S., HALIFAX, NOVA SCOTIA.

CHAPTER ELEVEN

Earning Their Keep: The Pay-For-Work Allowance System

✓ INTRODUCTION

One of the most concrete ways to teach children the value of money is to allow them to have some. Even very young children can grasp the basic principles of currency and how to earn, spend, and save it.

Figuring out what works for your family when it comes to whether to give allowances, how much and for what can be confusing. It seems every parenting or financial expert has a different idea of how parents should be setting up and administering a family monetary system. When deciding what works for you, keep in mind the purpose of giving an allowance: to give children hands-on experience with financial transactions. Any system that you set up that accomplishes that goal is worthwhile.

The Work-For-Pay allowance system meets that goal. It underlines the connection between effort and reward, which ultimately will be played out in the job market in later life. Under Work-For-Pay, kids can save for big purchases sooner if they want to put forth the effort to do more chores. It allows them to learn a skill that simply handing them money doesn't: how to prioritize "wants" by how much work has to be done to get them.

Handing children a fixed allowance every week and not tying it to effort leads to children believing that money is an entitlement. They will still view it as your money, not theirs and, therefore, are likely to treat it more casually than they would if they earned it from the sweat of their brow. It teaches kids that money does, in fact, grow on trees and that there will always be a steady supply of it. This lesson does not serve them well as they learn to handle their own finances.

✓ WHEN ARE KIDS OLD ENOUGH FOR AN ALLOWANCE?

Many parents choose to start an allowance system when their children start school, around ages six or seven. Waiting this long has its downsides, however. Kids begin to learn about money and about spending early, whether you teach it to them or not. They pick it up from television, from cartoons and toy advertisements; they find out what their friends are doing at school and play; and they start to try to figure it out on their own.

Teaching children good money habits early is imperative to starting them off in the right direction. Kids as young as three can recognize and distinguish the various values of coins and paper money. They can understand that money is what you get when you work for it, and they know that putting it in a piggy bank means they will have a growing amount of money. As soon as your kids are at this point, you can begin to set up an allowance system for them. Age-appropriate chores for young children are discussed later in this chapter.

✓ WHY KIDS NEED TO WORK FOR MONEY

There is no general consensus by "experts" on whether kids should work for money or simply be given it. Every family handles it differently. In a recent survey of 100 families across North America, 73 percent gave their kids some type of allowance. Only 32.5 percent (less than half of those who had an allowance scheme) had their children work for the money.

To understand why kids should have to work for pay, it's important to go back to the purpose of giving them allowance in the first place: to provide them with experience handling their own money. Giving kids a fixed amount of money every week does not teach them that money is something that requires effort and must be earned. Money is a scarce commodity and can't simply be withdrawn from the Bank of Mom and Dad.

Handing kids money weekly reinforces one of the Six Bad Money Habits: that there's always more where that came from. Instilling a work ethic and pride in earning their own money not only helps them learn that effort equals reward, it also changes the way they make their

The largest coin replica in the world is the Big Nickel in Sudbury, Ontario. It stands 30 feet high and is an almost perfect copy of a 1951 Canadian nickel. It is made from steel, not nickel.

> It frees you from doing things you dislike. Since I dislike doing nearly everything, money is handy.
> ~Groucho Marx

monetary value judgments. For example, it will be much harder for my daughter to choose to spend $50 on trendy shoes if she has to do jobs around the house for six hours to make that money rather than just automatically being given it. Spending—in the real world—always involves sacrifice, i.e., the other things you couldn't buy and the length of time it took to earn the money. This is an incredibly valuable lesson for kids to learn early.

Having said that, I am a firm believer that every family member, including kids, should contribute to the household just because they are a member of the family. There should always be certain expectations of each family member to keep the household running on a regular basis. I call these the Family Do's.

We pay our son between 2-3 dollars a week for chores. He has to keep his room clean and help when either his father or I ask him. When we are doing a large chore, we will sometimes offer a little extra money. Cleaning the garage might earn him an extra dollar.

I tend to let my son buy anything he wants if he has enough money. I think it is a lesson in short-term versus long-term savings. When he buys little Lego sets as soon as he has enough money, he will never be able to save for the big Lego sets.

~ LOKI M., CHICAGO, IL

✓ FAMILY DO'S

In our family, everyone has his or her own jobs and responsibilities. I do almost all of the grocery shopping, meal planning, and cooking—mostly because I enjoy doing it. I also manage school schedules, arrange vet trips for the cats, and pay all the bills. That's my role in the house. My husband takes out the garbage, helps with cleaning, and handles what we call "Maps & Machines." Anything to do with directions or maps, he has to handle. Anything electronic that is broken, needs to be assembled, or otherwise assessed is also firmly in his domain. My kids are expected to keep their rooms clean, do their own laundry, clean the cat litter and perform routine cleaning jobs. That is their contribution in exchange for a roof over their head. None of us expects to be compensated for these tasks. These jobs are, however, expected to be done on a regular basis to keep the *S.S. Mohr* afloat.

> Do not value money for any more nor any less than its worth; it is a good servant but a bad master.
> ~Alexandre Dumas fils, Camille, 1852

Setting up your Family Do's list will help your kids understand the difference between working for money and contributing to a family. The latter is not optional and teaching kids early about service to the household will help them when they move out on their own and, all of a sudden, have to start cleaning their own toilets and paying their own bills.

Family Do's (or "chores," if you still prefer the traditional vernacular) vary from family to family. One way to decide who does what is to start by listing out all the household tasks that need to be done regularly. Then, as a family, you can begin slotting each job into someone's responsibility list. If you can do it on a big white board or piece of paper, it will be easier for family members to visualize the amount of work each person has to complete. This will keep some balance in job loads and make sure that Mom, for example, doesn't end up with the lion's share of all the tasks if she also works full time.

Every family will have to decide for themselves how chores should be divided up. A stay-at-home mom, for example, may take on a heavier load as an equal contribution to dad who may work full-time outside the home or vice versa. If there has been tension in your family about who does how much of the household work, this exercise may bring inequities to light and help you sort out responsibilities to avoid arguments in the future. Once everyone knows what they are responsible for, you will see conflict lessen. As in every other aspect of family life, setting clear expectations and accountability makes daily life run more smoothly.

If you flip an American penny a thousand times, it will not land on tails 50 percent of the time, but closer to 51 percent. The side with the head weighs slightly more so it lands (literally) face-down more often than not.

So what should your kids' Family Do's be? In part, it will depend on their age. Even the youngest children can help with tasks like sweeping or picking up their toys. Older kids can take a more active role in household jobs, like helping to cook dinner or laundry. In our family, there are jobs nobody wants to do (like cleaning the cat litter box every day) and jobs that everyone wants to do (like collecting eggs from the henhouse). Your kids' Family Do's lists should be a combination of these things. Everyone has to do things they don't want to do— another important life lesson—but some chores don't have to be so disagreeable.

Some common household tasks that kids can accomplish are:

- Vacuuming
- Sweeping
- Loading and unloading the dishwasher
- Keeping a child's bathroom clean
- Setting and clearing the dinner table
- Their own laundry
- Washing their sheets and re-making their bed
- Sorting out their school backpacks every week
- Tidying their rooms
- Making their school lunches
- Dusting
- Walking the dog
- Feeding and caring for pets or livestock

> Those who believe money can do everything are frequently prepared to do everything for money.
> ~Author Unknown

When you have agreed as a family on who is responsible for which tasks (including Mom and Dad), post the list prominently and include weekly or daily check boxes so that everyone can be visibly accountable for their own Family Do's jobs.

To make sure that the Family Do's run smoothly and to avoid having to nag or constantly remind everyone of their jobs, take some time up front to establish time lines for each job and consequences for incomplete or poorly-done jobs.

What happens if kids don't do their Family Do's? In our family, it means that they can't get paid for other household work. The Family Do's represent the baseline of chores that have to get done before anything else can happen. If our kids want their weekly income, they first have to make sure they have met their basic responsibilities.

✓ DECIDE WHAT YOUR KIDS WILL BE RESPONSIBLE FOR PAYING

Once you have the Family Do's set up, it's time to look at what your kids can do for money. These are chores that are optional. If the kids want to make money, they can do them. If not, their lack of funds is their own concern.

The first consideration when trying to decide how many chores you will make available to your kids for money, and how much you will pay them for each task, is to figure out what they will be responsible for paying with their own money. This is once again a decision that is as individual as each family. Some families choose to require that the children pay for items such as school lunches, school supplies, clothes, and toys. Other families decide that the parents will provide the essentials and will only require kids to buy toys, games, and other accessories they really want.

> [T]hose who live by numbers can also perish by them and it is a terrifying thing to have an adding machine write an epitaph, either way.
> ~George J.W. Goodman, The Money Game

There's a happy medium in there that parents can strive for. In our family, we have decided that providing our kids with all their necessities such as meals, school supplies, and clothing is part of the family contract that they work for with the Family Do's. However, for example, if my son wants a $75 pair of Nike's rather than the $25 running shoes I was planning on buying him, he must pay the difference. The same goes for our daughter: if she wants to splurge on weekend dinners and movies out with her friends, that comes from her bank account. If she wants to have friends over for popcorn, a rental movie, and homemade pizza, we'll cover that.

✓ SETTING UP A WORK-FOR-PAY ALLOWANCE SYSTEM

Once you have decided what jobs are going to be covered under the Family Do's list, it's time to work on the list of what your kids can do for pay. These tasks are often those that aren't daily or weekly but need to be done less frequently.

I like to include both short jobs and those that are more involved and labor-intensive. This gives kids a variety of work that they can fit into their schedules. For example, your ten-year-old daughter may be able to fit in a half-hour of sweeping the deck after school but may have to leave longer jobs until the weekend.

Start by listing all of the tasks that you think your kids could handle along with an estimated completion time and any deadlines (for example, if the grass has to be cut before the dinner party on Saturday). Include some details of how the job must be completed, for example, what criteria you will use to determine if the task has been completed to your satisfaction. Kids often need this type of feedback to know if they are doing a good job. It also saves conflict afterwards if they think they've done what you have asked of them but you do not concur.

For example, if I add cleaning the den to the list, the job will include putting all video games away on the shelf, picking toys up off the floor and putting them away, dusting off the tables, wiping down the television screen, vacuuming the floor and all furniture, and fluffing the couch cushions. If one of these sub-tasks is not completed, I do not consider the job done and will not pay for it. Making my expectations clear up front makes the process go more smoothly.

The jobs on the work list should not be mandatory. This is where your children have the option of working and earning money or going without money. This reinforces the link between effort and reward. It also means that the jobs on the list will either be done by you or go undone if the kids choose not to complete them. Your list will be ever-changing as seasonal tasks become more or less important that particular week.

I don't give my children an allowance. As members of the family, they are expected to pitch in with whatever needs to be done. However, I will pay them for extra chores done above and beyond their normal chores. This way they aren't asking me how much they will be paid every time I ask them to do something. They can earn spending money by working for it and still have to do home chores just because they need doing, just like they will have to do as adults.

~ THERESA L., CREAL SPRINGS, ILLINOIS

✓ HOW MUCH SHOULD I PAY MY KIDS?

Assigning a dollar value to a chore is an art more than a science. Just like every family differs on how much the Tooth Fairy brings for a lost tooth, compensation for chores differs from family to family. When deciding how much to pay your kids for each chore, keep in mind the following criteria:

What other kids in your area are getting paid—if, for example, there are kids in the neighborhood advertising lawn cutting services for $10, it doesn't make sense to pay your son $5 to cut yours. Keep the payments at the prevailing rate for your part of the country.

What you expect your kids to pay for with their chore money—if you are going to have your kids pay for things such as all their clothes, school lunches, and school supplies, you will have to pay them more than if they only have to purchase "fun" things with their money. Decide what they will be responsible for before deciding on a dollar amount.

How time-consuming or complex a task is—jobs that take longer or involve more detail or effort should be compensated at a higher rate, just like in the "real" job market. As an example, moving boxes around in the attic takes more effort than walking the dog. Building a set of shelves is more complicated and takes longer than dusting. Make the tasks fairly compensated relative to each other.

✓ THE SAVINGS IMPERATIVE

We talk in detail in Chapter Five, "The Penny Jar: Teaching Kids About Saving Money," about teaching kids how to save money, but the basic premise bears repeating here. I strongly believe that kids benefit from forced savings. Teaching them from a young age to set aside a portion of all money coming in the door gets them into an automatic saving habit that will serve them well their whole lives.

Decide ahead of time what you will require your kids to do with the money they earn from doing jobs around the house. In our family, the kids must set aside 10 percent in a separate bank account. This money represents very long-term savings and cannot be used for purchases as a child. It can be used later in life for purchasing a car, college expenses, or even making a down-payment on a home. The other 90 percent can be used at my kids' discretion. As discussed in Chapter Five, I encourage my kids to apportion a monthly amount for charitable donations and to decide how much should be saved for larger purchases like bikes and iPods, and how much is discretionary spending money for things such as movies, books, or concerts.

Be clear with your kids, if this is your first foray into giving them money, about the savings component and how it will be handled. Chapter Five also discusses setting up separate bank accounts for savings.

Working for Pay: Age 3-9

Even the youngest kids can begin grasping the concept of working for money. Many parents wait until kids begin school to start giving an allowance but, by that time, a child starts to absorb information about money from school, television, and friends. Giving them a solid start on their financial education before they are swayed by outside influences will get them off on the right foot.

Tasks can be quick and simple for this age bracket and increase in time spent and complexity as the child gets older. Common chores in this age group include:

- sweeping
- dusting
- picking up toys
- setting the dinner table

Many parents find that kids are most willing to do chores in this age group and that they enjoy helping out as much as earning money. Unfortunately, our son never fit that mold and grumbled about chores from the time he was old enough to do them!

Working for Pay: Age 10-15

This is the age bracket where kids can be the most helpful. They are old enough to do a thorough job at most tasks and understand that doing it right the first time will save them from having to do it all over again. Consider giving kids in this group a variety of jobs that will have the secondary effect of teaching them skills that will be important to them later in life. For example, I began allowing my son to cook dinner once every two weeks and taught him some simple and inexpensive recipes. He will be able to take this skill to university and hopefully avoid eating out at fast food restaurants.

Queen Elizabeth II appears on all Canadian coinage by tradition to represent the constitutional monarchy. The reigning British monarch has appeared on Canada's coins since 1908, the year the Royal Canadian Mint began.

Here are some ideas for jobs in this age group:

- making meals
- thorough bedroom cleanings
- yard work (brush clearing, lawn mowing, weed pulling, etc.)
- spring or fall cleaning, including washing out cupboards, painting, cleaning windows, etc.
- assisting with grocery shopping

My children get allowance for completing household chores. We have four kids, ages varying from 7 –14, who earn allowance. The amount is based on their ages, although they all do the same chores, just rotated each week. However, we expect more out of our 14-year-old than we do the 7-year-old, which is how we justify the difference in dollar amounts. When it was just my kids (ages 5 and 7 then), I did an allowance based on specific chores. Dishes earned them 50 cents. Cleaning their room earned them a dollar. I prefer that method but, with four kids, it was harder to keep track!

~ HEATHER M., COOPERSTOWN, NORTH DAKOTA

Working for Pay: Age 16 and Up

Maintaining a Work-For-Pay system for children in this age bracket can be tricky. Many kids this age are working part time outside the home and are juggling high school, college entrance exams, volunteer jobs, and a social life. If your child has transitioned into a part-time job, make sure that they apply the lessons they learned from working at home, especially doing the job right the first time. Also, ensure that any savings requirement you have set up for them is maintained and applied to earnings from outside jobs. Working a "real" job is your children's first substantial step toward financial independence, and the lessons they learn in working at this age will affect how they treat money and employment for the rest of their lives.

If your teen still wants to participate, she can do practically anything you can do. Common jobs for older teens include:

- car detailing
- yard work that involves tools like pruners or axes
- meal planning and grocery shopping
- other errands if they are driving
- small building projects like wall repairs or building shelves

> Our kids get a $5 weekly allowance, which they receive only if they adequately complete their weekly chores. Once they've done that, it's theirs. Their chores rotate each week, so no one gets bored, and they each have one daily and one weekly job. So far, it works out very well for us. We keep a job chart on the fridge so everyone can keep track.
>
> ~ KIMBERLY M., LUTZ, FL

✓ ARE THERE TAX IMPLICATIONS IN GIVING MY KIDS MONEY?

In both Canada and the United States, there are tax rules that you need to be aware of when paying your kids to work around the house. In this section, we are discussing the money paid in allowance in exchange for chores, not any other transfers of money specifically for tax planning or income splitting purposes. If you are transferring substantial funds to your kids— for whatever reason—each year, it is wise to consult a Chartered Accountant or Certified Public Accountant who can advise you on your particular situation.

There are two main concepts that deal with the taxation of money transferred to kids: the gift tax and the "kiddie tax." The gift tax deals with the money that is transferred and the kiddie tax deals with the income earned on that money when it is saved.

Gift Taxes

In Canada, money earned by children from doing chores around the house is not considered a gift, nor is it considered earned income. This means that there are no tax implications to these transfers. However, the amount paid has to be reasonable under the circumstances. If the Canada Revenue Agency decides that the transfers are mainly for income-splitting purposes, kiddie tax rules (outlined below) may kick in.

In the United States, paying kids for chores is considered a gift no matter how hard the child worked for the money. A gift tax kicks in on such transfers but only if they total more than $13,000 per year per child. If you are paying your kids more than that to do chores, you should be seeking professional tax advice. There is a lifetime gifting and estate transfer exemption that might mean that you do not have to pay this gift tax. If the amount you're paying your kids is less than $13,000 (as it will be for the vast majority of families), you don't have to worry about gifting.

Kiddie Taxes

The "kiddie tax" is so-called in both countries and can have tax implications as your children's savings increase. The purpose of implementing the kiddie tax was to stop high-income parents from transferring income-producing assets to minor children and allowing income on those assets to be taxed at the child's much lower income tax rate. For example, without the kiddie tax, parents could give a child a $9,000 stock portfolio and all of the interest and capital gains would be taxed at the child's tax rate, which is often half or less than that of the parents. The kiddie tax removes the incentive to do this by taxing at least a portion of the income at the parents' highest marginal tax rate.

In Canada, the kiddie tax taxes all interest and dividend income on gifts to minor children (under 18) in the hands of the parent. Capital gains belong to the child and are taxed (or exempted from tax) in their hands. These rules only apply if the Canada Revenue Agency decides that the transfers are gifts rather than payment for chores. Keeping track of what you pay your kids and which chores they were paid for can help you avoid these sticky issues.

In the United States, the kiddie tax only applies to income levels over two times the dependent deduction ($1,900 in 2011). All income derived from gifts from parents over that limit is taxed at the parents' marginal tax rate. If your child has savings that generate investment income near these levels, it's a good idea to consult a CPA.

> If inflation continues to soar, you're going to have to work like a dog just to live like one.
> ~George Gobel

In summary, if you're paying your kids less than $13,000 a year for chores, there are no tax implications for either your kids or you in most cases.

✓ SUMMARY

- Kids can start learning about how to spend, save, and earn money as early as three years old.

- Kids who have to work for their disposable income learn life lessons that will guide them when they are out in the world on their own.

- Some chores should be assigned to children just for being a part of the household.

- How much you pay your kids for each chore depends on many criteria, including what they will have to pay for out of that money, how time-consuming or complex the task is, and what the prevailing rates are in your area of the country.

- Transferring large amounts of money to your children may have tax consequences.

KAREN'S STORY

If I could go back in time and teach my daughter good money habits, it would revolve around how to save more prudently. We taught her to save half her allowance, but we should have also added in any money she received as gifts, too.

My best advice for parents and kids is to save as much as you can now so the out-of-pocket costs for school won't be such a burden for them and those helping them pay for it all. Also, start their junior year in high school looking for scholarships; don't wait until they graduate high school. When they are in their senior year, they can start applying for any scholarships that fit into their field of studies or other areas they may be eligible for. Every little scholarship helps.

My daughter was still in college when she moved back home. As long as she went to college, she didn't have to pay room and board as long as she kept going. Now that she's done for the time being, she still lives at home and has chores she has to do in order to stay here since she doesn't have an income.

It was our daughter's responsibility to set up her student loans. She did have some money put back to help pay for some of her incidentals while attending college. We did pay for part of it from what we earned and used credit cards for some of it so we could track how much we were spending on books and fees. She worked part time during a semester as a proctor, which also helped her pay for even more of her college needs.

As long as she has money to pay for it, she can buy whatever she wants. If she expects us to pay for it, there is a spending limit or we do have to approve whether or not she gets what she asks for.

~ KAREN B., BELLE PLAINE, KS

CHAPTER TWELVE

Harnessing the Flow: Teaching Kids to Budget

✓ INTRODUCTION

Once your children understand the concepts of earning, saving, and spending money, they need to learn to formally budget their money. You may not see the need at first to show them how to write down every single dollar that comes and goes and to plan future spending down to the dollar. You may not be doing that yourself and, if that's the case, you are not alone. Over 50 percent of all families do not maintain a formal budget but over 80 percent of millionaire families do.

My grandmother used to say, "Take care of the nickels and dimes, and the dollars will take care of themselves." It's as true today as it was then. It simply means that if you pay attention to every small expense, your wealth will build automatically.

I've had many financial planning clients come to me for the first

> If you spent a thousand dollars every single day, it would take you 2,749 years to spend a billion dollars.

time for advice on complex tax and investing strategies in order to grow their savings. My first question is always, "Where's your budget?" It is often met with fidgeting or excuses as to why the client doesn't have time to write everything down. Many of these people are bleeding money every month—sometimes hundreds or even thousands of dollars—that slip through their hands without conscious thought. Just think, if you forego that $5 latte or breakfast burrito every morning on your way to work every day for a year, that's an extra $1,250 you have to invest in your retirement savings, or you could even take a vacation with the money. The nickels and dimes always add up to be dollars, and, often, lots of them.

> I am opposed to millionaires, but it would be dangerous to offer me the position.
> ~Mark Twain

When your children have their own money, either from allowance or from outside sources, the first step is determining how much should go into savings and donating (which we covered in earlier chapters) and how much should go to current spending. Budgeting helps kids focus on those purchases that will give them the most benefits versus other potential purchases.

The complexity of your children's budget will depend a lot on both their ages and their spending goals. Some kids save up their spending money for larger, and less frequent, purchases. Their budgets do not have to be so elaborate. However, if you have a teenager who likes to go out every weekend to the movies, the pizza place, and shopping, he will need to take more time to track and budget his expenses. The more time and care kids take to set up the initial budget, the easier it will be to follow and to stay on track.

✓ STEP 1: WRITING IT ALL DOWN

The first step in any budget is to know what you are really working with, not just what you think you spend. It's also usually the hardest step in the process. If kids are used to spending whatever is in their pocket, they might not have a good handle on where that money goes.

> It is the wretchedness of being rich that you have to live with rich people.
> ~Logan Pearsall Smith

Have your kids keep a journal and write down every purchase they make and all of the money coming in. It's not much different than keeping a check register that keeps a running balance. Have them do this for at least two months so that spending trends begin to manifest themselves. If you have never formalized your own budget, you can do this exercise alongside your kids. You may also be surprised how much money you are actually spending on frivolous things every month.

When the two months of tracking is over, the kids should add up all their expenses by type, for example, Entertainment, Clothes, Food, and School Supplies. Now we have some base information to make the budget more realistic.

✓ STEP 2: SETTING UP THE BUDGET

Putting together an actual budget can be very simple or very complex. Younger children can simply write down the 12 months of the year on a piece of paper and put into each month how much money they think they will get from allowance or other sources and how much they plan to spend in every month. The savings portion of their allowance can either go in the budget like any other expense or they can start out only with the net spending portion of the incoming money. I prefer an all-encompassing budget that shows all the money projected to come in and where all of it is planned to go, including savings, tithing, and donations.

Older children with some basic computer skills can set up the same information in a computerized spreadsheet, such as Microsoft Excel. The revenues and expenses can be written down the side and the months across the top. A spreadsheet can be set up to total both the rows and columns to make tracking a little easier. Kids eight and over can generally handle working with a simple spreadsheet. For older children (and adults), I recommend a software program like Quicken. There are many benefits of Quicken. You can track all of your actual income and spending as well as set up your budget. Then, it's as simple as running a report to check the actual totals as compared to the budget to see where you've missed the mark. There are also several other planning features that your kids can grow into as they start to manage their own financial affairs in the future. One example is the debt reduction planner that allows you to test different scenarios to pay down credit cards or mortgages faster.

My daughter is autistic. We have tried over and over to get her to understand the concept of money, bills, etc. I finally just sat down with her and made a list of all the bills and expenses for the month and then I showed her how much money we have coming in. She was finally able to understand that when I told her she couldn't get something, it wasn't that I was trying to be mean. We just couldn't afford it at that particular time. She is eleven.

~ HEATHER S., GREENSBORO, PENNSYLVANIA

✓ DISCRETIONARY VERSUS NON-DISCRETIONARY EXPENSES

When working on the budget, it's important for kids to understand the difference between discretionary and non-discretionary expenses. The vast majority of kids' spending is discretionary, meaning that they can choose to do it or not and they can choose the amount of the spending. Non-discretionary means that the money has to be spent. A grown-up example of a discretionary expense is entertainment. You don't have to spend money on entertainment (although it's always nice!). Even groceries have a discretionary component. You have to feed yourself (the non-discretionary part), but you don't have to buy filet mignon. Your grocery budget could be $200 a month or $800. You have some control over the amount. A non-discretionary expense would be car insurance. If you have a car, you need to pay insurance every month. You have no control over that expense in the short term. Discretionary expenses are much easier to adjust in a budget than non-discretionary.

> We live by the Golden Rule. Those who have the gold make the rules.
> ~Buzzie Bavasi

In a child's spending budget, an example of a non-discretionary expense would be cell-phone bills (if they have one) or committed monthly donations to charity. If the budget has to be adjusted down the road because it is continually lower than the actual spending, the discretionary items in the budget will need to be the first to be eligible for reducing.

✓ STEP 3: THE ENVELOPE METHOD

Once your children know how much they can spend every month and on what, the next step is to make sure the money is set aside for those purposes. If the budget is simple, the money can be left in the jar/piggy bank/savings account until it is needed. However, for multiple expenditures every month, I favor going back to a method most of our grandmothers used—the envelope.

The envelope method of budgeting and spending is very simple and easy to follow for kids. Once the total monthly spending budget has been set up, the money to fund it is apportioned between envelopes—one for every type of expense. For kids, it might be Toys, Comic Books, Jeans, and CDs. For adults, the envelopes would look more along the lines of Mortgage, Hydro, Telephone, etc. In the age of electronic payments, the envelope system no longer works as well for grown-ups, but it's still a very visual way for kids to learn to stay within their budgets. Once the money in the envelope is gone that month, there is no more spending allowed for that category.

I never really did much budgeting until a few months ago. I wanted to show my two girls how to be responsible with money and then realized that I wasn't being responsible. It was painful to start budgeting because I had to be accountable for every little thing I bought, right down to the magazines at the grocery store checkout. I'm glad I started, though, because it made me realize that even cutting back our expenses wasn't going to help enough. I had

✓ STEP 4: COMPARING WHAT HAPPENED TO WHAT SHOULD HAVE HAPPENED

This is the step that often both kids and adults stumble over. Without comparing the actual spending to the budgeted spending, setting up a budget is pointless. The envelope system makes this very easy for kids to grasp. If there's money left over in the envelopes at the end of the month, spending was less than the budget and they are on track. If the envelopes are all empty and they did not have enough money to do or buy the things they wanted to, then they overspent and they will have less to spend next month.

What happens when there is money left over in the envelopes at the end of the month? Some parents would insist that the money be put into savings, but I recommend that you allow your child to put the money into next month's spending budget for the same category. Otherwise, kids can develop the "if I don't spend it, I lose it" mentality. Even though it's in savings, they can't touch it, so it appears to be gone to them. It can force unnecessary and frivolous spending. (As a side note, the same thing happens frequently in municipal budgeting, where, if the money doesn't get spent, it gets lost.) If your child gets a deal on something or chooses not to buy something and, therefore, has money left over, she should be rewarded by being allowed to spend it later. This approach gives kids more discretion in the timing of spending and when they will get the most for their money. And that's the whole point of budgeting in the first place.

✓ STEP 5: RE-TOOLING THE BUDGET

Budgets are not a static, permanent set of figures. Everyone's life and priorities change and spending goals and needs must change accordingly. The final step of the budgeting process is to review it after several months of operating on it. Because almost all of a child's spending is discretionary, re-tooling the budget is a reasonably easy process. For example, if kids find that they are regularly spending more on clothes than they had allocated in the budget, and they wish to continue to do so, they will have to either increase the budgeted money coming in (by working more) or adjust the budget for another expense downward.

A rich man is nothing but a poor man with money.
~W.C. Fields

In a family budget, the changes are more complex. If the electricity bill is regularly 10 percent more than budget, the budget should change to reflect the realities of keeping the lights on. Because electricity is non-discretionary, it means reducing discretionary expenses, such as entertainment or vacations.

> *My kids know that money is tight. I'm a single mom and I explain to them honestly when money is really especially tight and they understand. They don't do a lot of begging for things and they actually pitch in their own money for special things they want to do rather than expect Mom to pay for it. I try not to burden them, but I also want them to understand that you have to work to earn money and, when you don't have enough money, you can't always do what you want—you have to wait or just not do it.*
>
> ~ TAMMY M., MARION, ILLINOIS

✓ SAMPLE BUDGET TEMPLATE FOR KIDS

MONTH

	1	2	3	4	5	6	7	8	9	10	11	12	Totals
MONEY COMING IN													
Allowance													
Other													
A. TOTAL INCOMING													
MONEY GOING OUT													
Donations													
Short-term savings													
Long-term savings													
Entertainment													
Clothes													
Other													
Other													
B. TOTAL OUTGOING													
C. SURPLUS (A-B)													
D. Total Surplus													

* Total surplus is the amount of surplus that you have carried over from previous months plus this month's surplus. If you have a negative surplus (called a deficit) in any month, you MUST have a total surplus from previous months enough to cover it. Otherwise, you do not have enough money to meet your spending goals.

My son is 14 and he not only budgets for himself, he helps me prepare the family budget every month. He has a good grasp of what we have coming in and going out and he's even suggested changes that really helped us. Right now, he's learning how to make the grocery budget go further and he plans out the meals for one week every month. Now, if I can just get him to cook them!

~ JULIA F., REGINA, SASKATCHEWAN

✓ SUMMARY

- Learning how to keep a running budget and tracking expenses early helps kids to formalize their financial planning when they go off into the world on their own.

- Budgets can be very simple for young children and more complex as spending increases. Computerized programs, such as Quicken, help with comparing actual spending to budgeted spending.

- Non-discretionary expenses are those that are fixed and unchangeable in the short term. Discretionary expenses are those that can be changed if the budget needs to be re-tooled.

- The final step in the budget process is reviewing the relevance and accuracy of the budget after working with it for several months. Budgets are not static and should be changed to reflect new expense realities.

- Children have few non-discretionary expenses, so changing their budgets to reflect what they actually spend money on is a reasonably simple process.

PATSY'S STORY

My daughter was 10 when we first set up a savings plan for her. The rule was that she had to save 10 percent and could spend the rest of her money on whatever she wanted.

She had a job all the way through high school—starting at 15. She applied and got the jobs all on her own. She worked at a local amusement park for 2 years (mainly summers) which was a great way to learn work ethics. They had a whole brochure on dress code, personal hygiene, what to do if you're sick, etc. Really broke the kids in! Then she worked at a shoe store.

After graduation, she could come home and live free for 6 months—adequate time to get on her feet. If she was still there after 6 months, room & board kicked in. I would base it on a percentage of her income.

As for college costs, I help pay about a third, financial aid pays about a third, and about a third is paid by her student loans. She has to work to have spending, gas, food, books, entertainment money, etc. She is working part time at the college and part time at a local retailer.

As a college student, her money is her money. I'll help pay tuition and occasionally books—and the flight home. But the rest? She needs to earn it. When she had moaned about it, I explained that I don't eat out, go dancing, or go to the movies all the time—so why should I work all the time and pay for her to do the things that I don't even do?

~ PATSY R., DENVER, COLORADO

CHAPTER THIRTEEN

Money Games: Fun Ways to Hone Your Kids' Money Smarts

✓ INTRODUCTION

Teaching kids about money isn't all about sitting them down and lecturing them. In fact, that approach has the least chance of being successful. Kids learn by what they see and hear you do and also by participating and practicing their money skills.

> It's a kind of spiritual snobbery that makes people think they can be happy without money.
> ~Albert Camus

Games are a great way to get kids interested in financial planning and budgeting. Most money games are really just scenario testing, i.e., getting kids to work through realistic financial scenarios and practice coming up with solutions. In fact, once your kids get to be 15 or so, they likely won't appreciate the word "games" but will be more interested in participating in real financial planning for the family.

I have split the games into rough age groups, but your children may be more or less math-oriented at certain ages. Adapt the games any way that you wish to keep your kids engaged and interested in the process.

✓ AGES 3-6

Dollar Builder

There are 242 combinations of change that equal a dollar, if you do not use half-dollar or dollar coins. For this game, pull out your change jar and have your child come up with a number of ways to make a dollar. A child who is just beginning to recognize the different coins may only be able to come up with four or five different combinations, but an older child may be able to come up with many more. Set a goal, such as 5 or 10 different ways but encourage your children to come up with extras. Some of the most common combinations are 4 quarters, 10 dimes, 20 nickels, 100 pennies, 2 quarters and 5 dimes, etc. As an extra incentive, you can allow children to keep the dollar combinations they come up with.

The Mom & Dad Store

This can be a one-time event or an ongoing game. If your children are already getting an allowance and have a designated spending portion, you can run your own little "tuck shop" where they can choose items from your store based on their available funds. They must calculate how much money they have and whether they have enough to buy what they want. The benefit of this for parents is that kids only have purchasing choices that you want them to have rather than taking them to a store and having to say "no" many times. The benefit for kids is that, not only do they get practice

The number 13, featured extensively on the American dollar bill, represents the original 13 colonies. On the bill, there are 13 steps on the pyramid, 13 stars above the eagle, 13 bars and 13 stripes on the shield, 13 leaves and 13 berries on the olive branch, 13 arrows, 13 letters in the Latin words Annuit Coeptis and E Pluribus Unum, and 13 hats. Finally, the number of characters in the year 1776 and its Latin form, MDCCLXXVI, equals 13.

counting and estimating, they can see the items regularly and may be more motivated to earn allowance to buy them. For kids that are starting to understand about taxes, be sure to calculate tax on top of the "sales price." Also, have older kids calculate how much change you need to give them back for the purchase.

Which Would You Rather Have?

This is a simple counting game that gets kids used to adding up money. You can use just change or both change and dollar bills for this game. The goal of the game is to choose the option that has the most total money. Set out two options on a table. For example, one option could be three quarters and the other option eight dimes. Ask them which they would rather have. If they choose the combination with the lower value, have them add up both piles again to determine which contains more money.

My kids love playing Monopoly and we play as a family at least weekly. To them, it's just a game, but it has taught them how to handle money and make change, how to budget purchases, and how to make money. I love that they know a fair bit about how real estate works and how to make deals. Now I just need to give them some real-life examples, using real money instead of play money.

~ ROBERTA P., SEATTLE, WASHINGTON

✓ AGES 7-9

The Grocery Store Game

This is a game that you can play with your kids and their friends if you want a little healthy competition. The goal of the game is to see how much food kids can buy for the food bank with $5. You will give each child a five-dollar bill. Before you go to the grocery store, let them peruse the weekly sales flyer to see if anything is on a particularly good sale. Give them a list of items that are appropriate for a food bank, such as spaghetti, spaghetti sauce, canned soup, beans, peanut butter, and canned chili. Then, take them to the store, give them their own cart (many stores have smaller-size carts that are easier for kids to maneuver), and let them spend their five dollars. They will need a pencil and paper at the least to keep track of the running total, but allow them to use calculators if they know how. Remind them of the tax implications in your area, if there are any, so that they can figure them into their budget. Let them check out with the cashier on their own and just monitor in case someone has miscalculated and goes over the five dollars. If that happens, stipulate that they must put something back. It's best to play this game when grocery stores aren't as busy, to reduce the stress on you, the kids, and the cashier! Whoever was able to buy the highest number of items for the food bank for their five dollars wins.

> O Gold! I still prefer thee unto paper,
> Which makes bank credit like a bark of vapour.
> ~Lord Byron

Store Owner

This game allows your children to virtually build their own store. Let them decide what they're going to sell (even if it is all gumballs!). Help them to walk through what they need to buy before they open the store and how much it will cost. If you have an Internet-savvy child, let her try to find real costs for some of the items, such as the wholesale cost of the product, the rent on the store, the cost of an employee, etc. The main goal is not to do a full business plan, but to contemplate everything that has to be budgeted for to run a store. For more inexperienced children, you can simply make up the costs. To be more realistic, choose a wholesale cost of around 50 percent of the retail cost. Ask your child to write down how she is going to get customers to come in the door (advertising) and how much she is going to have to sell in order to cover the costs (break even analysis). If your child is artistic, you can even get her to design a logo or sign for the business.

The Budgeting Game

This game develops your kids' planning and estimation skills. It is a precursor to developing their own actual budgets. The scenario is that they receive $20 a month (or $50 or whatever amount you choose). You also provide them with a list of things they can buy and what they cost. In this age group, make the items fun things that they would enjoy. The goal of the game is to figure out how to buy the most number of items on the list over the course of a year. This means that they will have to make purchases as they go and carry over any change to the next month until they have enough money to buy the next item. One rule is that they must make at least one purchase per month, so make sure your list includes items both under and over $20.

✓ AGES 10-14

Grocery Shopping Boss

Kids in this age group are ready to deal with more real-life money situations. This game allows them to be in charge of one grocery shopping trip. You will tell them what the budget of the entire trip is based on your own family budget. Give them a list of things that you absolutely need to buy. Allow them to look through the weekly sales flyer to see what's on sale and help them to choose a few things from the list that are useful and appropriate for your family. For example, if bread is on sale and someone in the family has gluten allergies, it would not fit with your lifestyle. Help your child finish the shopping list and write down approximate costs so that he knows he can stay within the budget. Then let him run the shopping trip. He will have to shop only by the list and keep a running total of purchases. Give him the money ahead of time and let him check out with minimal supervision.

Standard editions of the game Monopoly have $15,140 in the bank, consisting of twenty $500 bills, twenty $100 bills, thirty $50 bills, fifty $20 bills, forty $10 bills, forty $5 bills, and forty $1 bills.

Monopoly

This real estate game has been around since 1935 and is still an excellent teaching tool for kids. Monopoly teaches estimation skills, business skills, and bartering skills. There are many versions of the game out there, including junior versions, which are simplified and easier for younger children to navigate. If you are using a regular Monopoly game with children, you can dole out half of the stated amount of money to shorten the game.

The waste of money cures itself, for soon there is no more to waste.
~M.W. Harrison

The Budgeting Game II

Kids in this age group can start practicing with more realistic budgets. Give them a scenario that looks more like your family's budget. Establish the amount of income coming in every month, perhaps $1,500 to $3,000, and all of the expenses that need to be paid. To make it more sophisticated, add in debt, so that your kids can see that they have to pay interest on that debt from the income every month, but, if they apply some of the surplus every month to pay down the debt, they will have less interest to pay going forward. You can make this scenario as simple or complicated as you wish. You can even use your own family budget as a starter.

When my kids were little, we used to play our version of the Grocery Store Game. Each was given a few items on our grocery list that they were responsible for finding and getting the best price on. They loved it when I handed them coupons for the item, too. My daughter is 19 now and my son is 18. Both of them are pretty shrewd shoppers and both love cutting coupons!

~ CATHY N., QUEBEC CITY, QUEBEC

✓ AGES 15 AND UP

Food Budget Boss

To begin preparing your kids for their eventual nest-leaving, let them dip their toes in real-world budgeting and planning. Let your child take over the grocery budget for the month. This means that you tell her what the monthly budget is and it is her job to plan out all the family meals for the month, calculate their approximate costs, and do the shopping. For example, if your grocery budget is $400 for the month, your child will have to estimate that she has around $13 a day for family meals. She will have to come up with meals that fit that budget. If she doesn't have a lot of cooking experience, you will have to help with approximate portion sizes needed, etc. For example, if she's budgeting a quarter pound of hamburger for a dinner for four, that probably won't work. Help her plan out the meals so that there is variety and nutrition (30 dinners of spaghetti and meatballs won't cut it). Then, let her do the grocery shopping required for the month. This might be done in a single trip but more likely weekly trips, which will require more planning. This is a great exercise in stretching a budget.

Car Insurance Comparison

Comparison shopping is an important skill to develop. When kids are young, they can comparison shop at the grocery store. Older kids can start assessing larger expenses. Car insurance is a great expense to try to reduce as everyone should be assessing their insurance options on a regular basis anyway. Show your child your insurance policy, including what it costs and what it will pay out. Explain that the benefits of the policy cannot change (i.e., getting a cheaper price for fewer benefits doesn't count). Also, explain that only solid companies should be compared. A quote from a less-reputable company may be cheaper, but the service may be worse and the company may not pay out if there is a claim. You can even give him a list of companies to compare. After he has done his research, he can present his findings to you and recommend staying with the current provider or switching. You may even find an insurance deal from the exercise!

> I'm so poor I can't even pay attention.
> ~Ron Kittle, 1987

Vacation Planning

This is another useful scenario that could actually lead to a great family vacation for a lot less. Let your teen do the research and plan it. Give her the parameters, for example, how long it should be, what the overall budget should be, and roughly where you want to go. Then let her investigate all the options. She can compare rental car prices, hotels only versus all-inclusives, airfares, etc., to be able to get the most for the least. Even if you don't ultimately go with her recommendation, you will both have learned more about finding the best deals.

✓ SUMMARY

- Teaching kids money skills through games and exercises is a great way for them to practice their financial wisdom.

- Kids from 3-6 should start by practicing their coin recognition and adding skills.

- Kids from 7-9 have more experience with handling money and can start practicing their budgeting skills.

- 10–14-year-olds can start learning more real-world situations by helping with grocery budgeting.

- By age 15, the word "game" really doesn't apply anymore, but kids can do basic research and comparison-shopping exercises for the family.

LISA'S STORY

Our kids know our entire household budget. We go over it together so they can understand how much it costs to make a family work and how we budget that money to cover the necessities and have enough left for family fun. We allow them to help plan by showing them our budgets for fun and food and asking them to help us plan meals and activities that stay in budget. Now they understand why we can't go to Six Flags every weekend.

We have to approve of their purchases (they are only 10 and 12). Small purchases of their own money can be made as soon as they see it. For larger purchases, we ask them to "sleep on it." They often change their mind about what they want to buy when they have had time to think on it. We do pro and con lists for big purchases, too. My daughter hoards money for months and then spends it in a heartbeat (often on other people) without really thinking or caring about it. My son wants to spend right away rather than hold onto the money, but he calculates down to every penny so he can get the absolute most for his dollars. We are teaching them about their "spending personalities" and how to be responsible with their money but still enjoy it. If our kids wanted to come back home as adults, they would pay a percentage of the expenses like a "roommate" or renter unless there was an emergency such as a medical problem or accident that incapacitated them. The goal would be to get them back on their feet and out on their own in a reasonable time frame, so we would discuss how long they could stay before they came back home to live. I love my kids dearly and want to be part of their lives forever but learning to be self-reliant is important. It's my job to help teach them that.

~ LISA M., AUSTIN, TEXAS

MONEY WORDS

Accrued Interest—the interest on a bond or other fixed-income security that has been earned over time but not yet paid out.

Ad Valorem Taxes—a tax based on the value of a piece of property. The term is not commonly used in Canada, but is often imposed in the United States on car tag renewals, rather than a flat renewal fee. Property taxes on real estate are technically ad valorem taxes but are more frequently identified by the former term.

Annual Percentage Rate (APR)—the percentage interest rate paid on a loan over a year, including fees and other costs.

Annuities—an investment that grows over time and then pays out a stream of payments over time to the investor.

Asset—what you own, including property, vehicles, investments, patents, and other items of value.

ATM—Automated Teller Machine. These machines may be owned by banks or private companies, from which you can access funds from your bank account around the clock.

Balanced funds—hybrid mutual funds that contain both stocks and bonds to provide investors with growth and income with a lower overall risk than either individual investment.

Bank card—also called an ATM or debit card. This plastic card looks like a credit card, but it is used to withdraw money from a savings or checking account.

Billionaire—a person whose net worth (assets minus liabilities) is equal to a billion dollars or more.

Bond—a note issued by a corporation or government that confirms you are lending the corporation or government money. Bonds pay interest regularly to investors. At the end of the term of the bond, the borrower returns to the lender the face value of the bond (the amount the lender invested in the bond) plus any accrued interest.

Capital gains—profit from an increase in the underlying value of an investment.

CDIC–Canada Deposit Insurance Corporation—a federal corporation that protects the deposits of investors held in banks up to a certain limit.

Certificate of Deposit (CD)—a type of investment in the U.S. that requires you to invest money for a locked-in period of time and guarantees the same rate of return (interest) for that entire time. CDs usually require a minimum deposit.

Chequing (checking) account—a bank account used for the purpose of making easy transactions, as opposed to an account used for savings or for earning interest.

Compound interest—interest that accumulates on an investment where future interest is calculated on both the initial investment and the accumulated interest.

Credit—a loan that gives people access to funds now to be repaid in the future.

Credit report—a history of a person's dealings with credit, including repayments and the total amount of debt still owed.

Credit score—a value assigned to your credit history by credit bureaus to summarize your credit-worthiness.

Debt—what you owe to others.

Debt consolidation—converting your existing debt into a new loan.

Direct deposit—an automatic electronic deposit to a bank account, often by employers for paychecks.

Disability Insurance—provides either short-term or long-term income in the event of illness or injury that prevents you from working.

Discretionary expenses—expenses over which you have some control as to the timing or the amount of the spending.

Diversification—investing in a variety of different assets in order to spread out the risk.

Dividends—regular investment returns paid to the owners (shareholders) of a corporation from the net profit of the company.

Down payment—a preliminary payment on a large purchase, the rest of which will be financed over time.

Earned income—income that requires continuing time and effort to obtain.

Employment insurance premiums—premiums paid by an employer or employee to a fund that pays employees who become unemployed or, in some places, go on maternity or parental leave.

Entrepreneur—a person who plans and starts up a business in order to grow it to profit either from its operations or its sale.

Expenses—money paid out for things that people want or need.

Face value—the amount a bond was originally issued for and the amount it will be redeemed for.

FDIC–Federal Deposit Insurance Corporation—a U.S. federal organization that was established under the Banking Act of 1933. It protects the deposits of investors held in banks up to a certain limit.

Financial statements—a summarization of the financial activity of a company or person over a period of time.

Foreclosure—a legal process in which a lender can take custody of an asset of a borrower in the even of a default on the loan.

GIC–Guaranteed Investment Certificate—a Canadian fixed-income investment much like a U.S. Certificate of Deposit. GICs pay interest and are backed by the overall reputation of the bank issuing them.

Gross pay—the total income on a paycheck based on your agreed salary or hourly wage before any deductions have been subtracted.

Health insurance—a type of insurance that pays for medical costs, which could include doctors, hospitals, or prescription drugs.

Home equity—the net difference between the current value of a house and all mortgages, loans, or other encumbrances against it.

Homeowner's insurance—insurance that covers damage to a home from fire, theft, or some other calamities, depending on the policy. Sometimes also covers medical costs for those who hurt themselves on the property.

Income tax—a tax on individual and business income used by the government to provide infrastructure and social programs.

Insurance—a contract between an insurance company and a policyholder that protects against specific financial losses, such as death, health, disability, or property damage.

Interest—the premium paid by a borrower to an investor for a loan.

Interest Rate—the price paid for the use of someone else's money expressed as an annual percentage rate, such as 6.5%.

Investment—using your money to try to make more money—for example, by depositing money in a bank or by buying a bond or stock in a company.

Junk Bonds—bonds issued by entities that are rated BB or below. This makes them high risk. They offer a higher rate of return because they are at a higher risk of default.

Leverage—the use of debt to gain assets with the intention that the assets will increase and the debt will decrease over time.

Life insurance—an insurance policy that pays money to the heirs of the policyholder on death.

Lifetime Financial Plan—an overall financial map for every stage of life, including the milestones of adulthood, university or college, home ownership, retirement, and death.

Loan—money given for a period of time by a lender to a borrower, with a contract stating the timing of the return of the initial money plus any interest.

Long-Term—looking to the future. In the context of savings, it means money that does not have to be used for a long period of time.

Macroeconomics—the study of how governments interact with each other and how government policy impacts things like interest rates, employment, and inflation.

Microeconomics—the study of the financial interactions between consumers and companies and how they affect things like pricing and demand for goods and services.

Millionaire—a person whose net worth (assets minus liabilities) is equal to a million dollars or more.

Mortgage—a loan on real property, such as a house or land, that often is a long-term loan secured by the property.

Mutual funds—funds that invest in stocks, bonds, and other individual investments and sell units of ownership to investors.

Net pay—the amount of a paycheck that you actually get to take home after all deductions have been taken (also called take-home pay).

Net worth—amount of assets one owns over the debts one owes.

Non-discretionary expenses—expenses over which you have little or no control over the amount or timing of payment in the short term.

NSF—stands for non-sufficient funds; a term used by banks when they decline a transaction presented to your account because there is not enough money in the account to cover it.

Opportunity cost—the value of what you give up by making an alternate choice.

Overdrawn—a situation where you withdraw more money from your bank account than you have in there. It is basically a short-term loan from the bank that must be repaid quickly and usually incurs significant fees.

Passive income—regular income that requires little or no ongoing effort; examples include rental income, royalties, interest, or pensions.

Penny stock—a common term for stocks on the stock market that are valued at less than a dollar per share. These are usually start-up companies or companies for which there are few assets. They are highly speculative and go down to zero much more often than they go up in value.

Premiums—usually refers to the regular payments made on an insurance policy.

Principal—the original amount of a loan without any interest or other fees.

Profit—used in business to represent the net amount of income after all expenses have been deducted from the revenues of the company. The profit is what is available to go to the owners of the company or to be re-invested.

Property and casualty insurance—insurance related to objects rather than people. Examples include homeowner's insurance, business interruption insurance, or professional liability insurance.

Real estate—tangible property, usually land and buildings.

Registered charity—a non-profit organization that may receive tax exemptions.

Retirement account—a savings or investment account for use when a person retires, or stops working. It often qualifies for tax advantages or exemptions.

Return—the amount of money an investor receives from an investment. The return on investment is often expressed as a percentage. The higher the risk of the investment, the higher the return is likely to be.

Risk—the likelihood that you will lose money on an investment. There are many different kinds of risk in investments, such as interest rate risk and foreign currency risk.

Savings account—a bank account meant for keeping money for a longer period of time than a checking account. Savings accounts often pay higher interest but do not have checks with which to withdraw money or pay bills.

Short-Term—a small time horizon. In savings, it refers to the fact that the money will be needed soon to spend.

Small business—a privately-owned business with relatively small staffing and sales volume.

Stock market—an organized exchange, or trading post, where investments can be bought and sold by individual investors or investment houses working on their behalf. The price of each stock rises and falls in real time as trades are made, based on volume and demand.

Tithing—giving money to the church or to a church-connected organization, based on the teachings of the church. Tithing is formalized in some churches and represents a percentage of one's income, usually 10 percent.

Withholding taxes—income and other taxes that are kept back by an employer from an employee's paycheck in order to remit directly to the government on the employee's behalf. The employee gets credit for these amounts already paid when the employee prepares her income tax return.

RESOURCES

1. **www.ixl.com**

   This educational site has both free and paid resources. It gives online training in math, money skills, and all kinds of other curriculum.

2. **www.investopedia.com**

   This site is chock-full of articles on personal finance. A great refresher for adults and an easy-to-understand source for kids.

3. **Financial Management 101–Angie Mohr, Self-Counsel Press (2008)**

   This book is part of my Numbers 101 for Small Business series and explains financial statements and what they tell small business owners. For teens who are serious about starting a business, it is a useful resource.

4. **www. piggybanks2paychecks.com**

   This is the official Web site for this book. Here you'll find lots more tools to help you and your kids learn money skills. There are downloadable worksheets, lesson plans, and more money games!

5. **www.msgen.com**

   Susan Beacham's fantastic "Money Savvy Generation" Web site. Susan offers all kinds of products to help kids grow their money skills, including savings banks and personal finance organizers.

MONEY RESOURCES FOR CANADIANS

1. **www.paypal.ca**

   PayPal's official site that includes lists of their products and services.

2. **www.quicken.ca**

   Quicken's Canadian site that provides comparisons of all of their financial management software.

3. **www.practicalmoneyskills.ca**

   This site was set up by Visa to provide a Canadian-focused set of resources for teachers, parents, and students. There are articles, games, and calculators, all about personal finance and money management.

4. **http://www.ic.gc.ca/eic/site/bsf-osb.nsf/eng/h_br01548.html**

   This is a part of the Office of the Superintendent of Bankruptcy Canada site. There are several guides here for kids of various ages that discuss the basics of finances, credit, and debt.

MONEY RESOURCES FOR AMERICANS

1. **www.quicken.com**

   Lots of great articles and resources for managing your money. You can also purchase and download Quicken personal financial software from the site.

2. **www.paypal.com**

   PayPal's website with a list of products and services available. In the United States, parents can set up a student account for their children who are 13 and over.

3. **www.usmint.gov/kids/games**

   The U.S. Mint has a great site with lots of money-related online games for kids up to about 12 years old. In other areas on the site, kids will find out how money is minted and the history of money.

4. **www.themint.org**

   This is an education foundation connected to Northwestern Mutual. There are sections for kids, teens, parents, and teachers, including quizzes and financial calculators.

INDEX